Modern Cookery in All Its Branches

Easy and Delicious Recipes

- Mary W. Cowan -

SWEETMEATS.

GENERAL REMARKS.

The introduction of iron ware lined with porcelain has fortunately almost superseded the use of brass or bell-metal kettles for boiling sweetmeats; a practice by which the articles prepared in those pernicious utensils were always more or less imbued with the deleterious qualities of the verdigris that is produced in them by the action of acids.

Charcoal furnaces will be found very convenient for preserving; the kettles being set on the top. They can be used in the open air. Sweetmeats should be boiled rather quickly, that the watery particles may exhale at once, without being subjected to so long a process as to spoil the colour and diminish the flavour of the fruit. But on the other hand, if boiled too short a time they will not keep so well.

If you wish your sweetmeats to look bright and clear, use only the very best loaf-sugar. Fruit may be preserved for family use and for common purposes, in sugar of inferior quality, but it will never have a good appearance, and it is also more liable to spoil.

If too small a proportion of sugar is allowed to the fruit, it will *certainly* not keep well. When this experiment is tried it is generally found to be false economy; as sweetmeats, when they begin to spoil, can only be recovered and made eatable by boiling them over again with additional sugar; and even then, they are never so good as if done properly at first. If jellies have not sufficient sugar, they do not congeal, but will remain liquid.

Jelly bags should be made of white flannel. It is well to have a wooden stand or frame like a towel horse, to which the bag can be tied while it is dripping. The bag should first be dipped in hot water, for if dry it will absorb too much of the juice. After the liquor is all in, close the top of the bag, that none of the flavour may evaporate.

In putting away sweetmeats, it is best to place them in small jars, as the more frequently they are exposed to the air by opening the more danger there is of their spoiling. The best vessels for this purpose are white queen's-ware pots, or glass jars. For jellies, jams, and for small fruit, common glass tumblers are very convenient, and may be covered simply with double tissue-paper, cut exactly to fit the inside of the top of the glass, laid lightly on the sweetmeat, and pressed down all round with the finger. This covering, if closely and nicely fitted, will be found to keep them perfectly well, and as it adheres so closely as to form a complete coat over the top, it is better for jellies or jams than writing-paper dipped in brandy, which is always somewhat shrivelled by the liquor with which it has been saturated.

If you find that your sweetmeats have become dry and candied, you may liquefy them again by setting the jars in water and making it boil round them.

In preserving fruit whole, it is best to put it first in a thin syrup. If boiled in a thick syrup at the beginning, the juice will be drawn out so as to shrink the fruit.

It is better to boil it but a short time at once, and then to take it out and let it get cold, afterwards returning it to the syrup, than to keep it boiling; too long at a time, which will cause it to break and lose its shape.

Preserving kettles should be rather broad than deep, for the fruit cannot be done equally if it is too much heaped. They should all have covers belonging to them, to put on after the scum has done rising that the flavour of the fruit may be kept in with the steam.

A perforated skimmer pierced all through with holes is a very necessary utensil in making sweetmeats.

The water used for melting the sugar should be very clear; spring or pump water is best. but if you are obliged to use river water, let it first be filtered. Any turbidness or impurity in the water will injure the clearness of the sweetmeats.

If sweetmeats ferment in the jars, boil them over again with additional sugar.

CLARIFIED SUGAR SYRUP.

Take eight pounds of the best double-refined loaf-sugar, and break it up or powder it. Have ready the whites of two eggs, beaten to a strong froth. Stir the white of egg gradually into two quarts of very clear spring or pump water. Put the sugar into a porcelain kettle, and mix with it the water and white of egg. While the sugar is melting, stir it frequently; and when it is entirely dissolved, put the kettle over a moderate fire, and let it boil, carefully taking off the scum as it comes to the top, and pouring in a little cold water when you find the syrup rising so as to run over the edge of the kettle. It will be well when it first boils hard to pour in half a pint of cold water to keep down the bubbles so that the scum may appear, and be easily removed. You must not however boil it to candy height, so that the bubbles will look like hard pearls, and the syrup will harden in the spoon and hang from it in strings; for though very thick and clear it must continue liquid. When it is done, let it stand till it gets quite cold; and if you do not want it for immediate use, put it into bottles and seal the corks.

When you wish to use this syrup for preserving, you have only to put the fruit into it, and boil it till tender and clear, but not till it breaks. Large fruit that is done whole, should first be boiled tender in a very thin syrup that it may not shrink. Small fruit, such as raspberries, strawberries, grapes, currants, gooseberries, &c. may, if perfectly ripe, be put raw into strong cold sugar syrup; they will thus retain their form and colour, and then freshness and natural taste. They must be put into small glass jars, and kept well covered with the syrup. This, however, is an experiment which sometimes fails, and had best be tried on a scale, or only for immediate use.

TO PRESERVE GINGER.

Take root of green ginger, and pare it neatly with a sharp knife, throwing it into a pan of cold water as you pare it. Then boil it till tender all through, changing the water three times. Each time put on the ginger is quite cold water to lake out the excessive heat. When it is perfectly tender, throw it again into a pan of cold water, and let it lie an hour or more; this will make it crisp. In the mean time prepare the syrup. For every six pounds of ginger root, clarify seven pounds of the best double-refined loaf-sugar. Break up the sugar, put it into a preserving kettle, and melt it in spring or pump water, (into which you have stirred gradually the beaten white of two eggs,) allowing a pint of water to each pound of sugar. Boil and skim it well. Then let the syrup stand till it is cold; and having drained the ginger, pour the syrup over it, cover it, and do not disturb it for two days. Then, having poured it from the ginger, boil the syrup over again. As soon as it is cold, pour it again on the ginger, and let it stand at least three days. Afterwards boil the syrup again, and pour it *hot* over the ginger. Proceed in this manner till you find that the syrup has thoroughly penetrated the ginger, (which you may ascertain by its taste and appearance when you cut a piece off,) and till the syrup becomes very thick and rich. Then put it all into jars, and cover it closely.

If you put the syrup hot to the ginger at first, it will shrink and shrivel. After the first time, you have only to boil and reboil the syrup; as it is not probable that it will require any further clarifying if carefully skimmed. It will be greatly improved by adding some lemon-juice at the close of the last boiling.

TO PRESERVE CITRONS.

Pare off the outer skin of some fine citrons, and cut them into quarters. Take out the middle. You may divide each quarter into several pieces. Lay them for four or five hours in salt and water. Take them out, and then soak them in spring or pump water (changing it frequently) till all the saltness is extracted, and till the last water tastes perfectly fresh. Boil a small lump of alum, and scald them in the alum-water. It must be very weak, or it will communicate an unpleasant taste to the citrons; a lump the size of a hickory nut will suffice for six pounds. Afterwards simmer them two hours with layers of green vine leaves. Then make a syrup, allowing a pint of water to each pound of loaf-sugar; boil and skim it well. When it is quite clear, put in the citrons, and boil them slowly, till they are so soft that a straw will pierce through them without breaking. Afterwards put them into a large dish, and set them in the sun to harden.

Prepare some lemons, by paring off the yellow rind very thin, and cutting it into slips of uniform size and shape. Lay the lemon-rind in scalding water, to extract the bitterness. Then take the pared lemons, cut them into quarters, measure a half pint of water to each lemon, and boil them to a mash. Strain the boiled lemon through a sieve, and to each pint of liquid allow a pound of the best double-refined loaf-sugar, for the second syrup. Melt the sugar in the liquid, and stir into it gradually some beaten white of egg; allowing one white to four pounds of sugar. Then set it over the fire; put the lemon-peel into the syrup, and let it boil in it till quite soft. Put the citrons cold into a glass jar, and pour the hot syrup over them. Let the lemon remain with the citrons, as it will improve their flavour.

If you wish the citrons to be candied, boil down the second syrup to candy height, (that is, till it hangs in strings from the spoon,) and pour it over the citrons. Keep them well covered. You may, if you choose, after you take the citrons from the alum-water, give them a boil in very weak ginger tea, made of the roots of green ginger if you can procure it; if not, of race ginger. Powdered ginger will not do at all. This ginger tea will completely eradicate any remaining taste of the salt or the alum. Afterwards cover the sides and bottom of the pan with vine leaves, put a layer of leaves between each layer of citron, and cover the top with leaves. Simmer the citrons in this two hours to green them.

In the same manner you may preserve water-melon rind, or the rind of cantelopes. Cut these rinds into stars, diamonds, crescents, circles, or into any fanciful shape you choose. Be sure to pare off the outside skin before you put the rinds into the salt and water.

Pumpkin cut into slips, may be preserved according to the above receipt.

CANTELOPES OR MUSK-MELONS.

Take very small cantelopes before they are ripe. Shave a thin paring off the whole outside. Cut out a small piece or plug about an inch square, and through it extract all the seeds, &c. from the middle. Then, return the plugs to the hole from whence you took them, and secure them with a needle and thread, or by tying a small string round the cantelope.

Lay the cantelopes for four or five hours in salt and water. Then put them into spring water to extract the salt, changing the water till you find it salt no longer. Scald them in weak alum-water. Make a syrup in the proportion of a pint of water to a pound of loaf-sugar, and boil the cantelopes in it till a straw will go through them. Then take them out, and set them in the sun to harden.

Prepare some fine ripe oranges, paring off the yellow rind very thin, and cutting it into slips, and then laying it in scalding water to extract the bitterness. Cut the oranges into pieces; allow a pint of water to each orange, and boil them to a pulp. Afterwards strain them, and allow to each pint of the liquid, a pound of the best loaf-sugar, and stir in a little beaten white of egg; one white to four pounds of sugar. This is for the second syrup. Boil the peel in it, skimming it well. When the peel is soft, take it all out; for if left among the cantelopes, it will communicate to it too strong a taste of the orange.

Put the cantelopes into your jars, and pour over them the hot syrup. Cover them closely, and keep them in a dry cool place.

Large cantelopes may be prepared for preserving (after you have taken off the outer rind) by cutting them into pieces according to the natural divisions with which they are fluted. This receipt for preserving cantelopes whole, will do very well for green lemons or limes, substituting lemon-peel and lemon-juice for that of oranges in the second syrup.

You may use some of the first syrup to boil up the pulp of the orange or lemons that has been left. It will make a sort of marmalade, that is very good for colds.

PRESERVED WATER-MELON RIND.

Having pared off the green skin, cut the rind of a water-melon into pieces of any shape you please; stars, diamonds, circles, crescents or leaves, using for the purpose a sharp penknife. Weigh the pieces, and allow to each pound a pound and a half of loaf sugar. Set the sugar aside, and put the pieces of melon-rind into a preserving kettle, the bottom and sides of which you, have lined with green vine leaves. Put a layer of vine leaves between each, layer of melon-rind, and cover the top with leaves. Disperse among the pieces some very small bits of alum, each about the bigness of a grain of corn, and allowing one bit to every pound of the melon-rind. Pour in just water enough to cover the whole, and place a thick double cloth (or some other covering) over the top of the kettle to keep in the steam, which will improve the greening. Let it simmer (but not boil) for two hours. Then take out the pieces of melon-rind and spread them on dishes to cool. Afterwards if you find that they taste of the alum, simmer them in very weak ginger tea for about three hours. Then proceed to make your syrup. Melt the sugar in clear spring or pump water, allowing a pint of water to a pound and a half of sugar, and mixing in with it some white of egg beaten to a stiff froth. The white of one egg will be enough for four pounds of sugar. Boil and skim it;

and when the scum ceases to rise, put in the melon-rind, and let it simmer an hour. Take it out and spread it to cool on dishes return it to the syrup, and simmer it another hour. After this take it out, and put it into a tureen. Boil up the syrup again, and pour it over the melon-rind. Cover it, and let it stand all night. Next morning give the syrup another boil; adding to It some lemon-juice, allowing the juice of one lemon to a quart of the syrup. When you find it so thick as to hang in a drop on the point of the spoon, it is sufficiently done. Then put the rind into glass jars, pour in the syrup, and secure the sweetmeats closely from the air with paper dipped in brandy, and a leather outer cover.

This, if carefully done and well greened, is a very nice sweetmeat, and may be used to ornament the top of creams, jellies, jams by laying it round in rings or wreaths.

Citrons may be preserved green in the same manner, first paring off the outer skin and cutting them into quarters. Also green limes.

PRESERVED PEPPERS.

For this purpose take the small round peppers while they are green. With a sharp penknife extract the seeds and cores; and then put the outsides into a kettle with vine leaves, and a little alum to give them firmness, and assist in keeping them green. Proceed precisely as directed for the water-melon rind, in the above receipt.

PUMPKIN CHIPS.

It is best to defer making this sweetmeat (which will be found very fine) till late in the season when lemons are ripe and are to be had in plenty. Pumpkins (as they keep well) can generally be procured at any time through the winter.

Take a fine pumpkin, of a rich deep colour, pare off the outer rind; remove the seeds; and having sliced the best part, cut it into chips of equal size, and about as thick as a half dollar. They should be in long narrow pieces, two inches in breadth, and six in length. It is best to prepare the pumpkin the day before; and having weighed the chips, allow to each pound of them a pound of the best loaf-sugar. You must have several dozen of fine ripe lemons, sufficient to furnish a jill of lemon-juice to each pound of pumpkin. Having rolled them under your hand on a table, to make them yield as much juice as possible, pare off the yellow rind and put it away for some other purpose. Then having cut the lemons, squeeze out all the juice into a pitcher. Lay the pumpkin chips in a large pan or tureen, strewing the sugar among them. Then having measured the lemon-juice in a wine-glass, (two common wine-glasses making one jill,) pour it over the pumpkin and sugar, cover the vessel, and let it stand all night.

Next day transfer the pumpkin, sugar, and lemon-juice to n preserving kettle, and boil it slowly three quarters of an hour, or till the pumpkin becomes all through tender, crisp, and transparent; but it must not be over the fire long enough to break and lose its form. You must skim it thoroughly. Some very small pieces of the lemon-paring may be boiled with it. When you think it is done, take up the pumpkin chips in a perforated skimmer that the syrup may drain through the holes back into the kettle. Spread the chips to cool on large dishes, and pass the syrup through a flannel bag that has been first dipped in hot water. When the chips are cold, put them into glass jars or tumblers, pour in the syrup, and lay on the top white paper dipped in brandy. Then tie up the jars with leather, or with covers of thick white paper.

If you find that when cold the chips are not perfectly clear, crisp, and tender, give them another boil in the syrup before you put them up.

This, if well made, is a handsome and excellent sweetmeat It need not be eaten with cream, the syrup being so delicious as to require nothing to improve it. Shells of puff-paste first baked empty, and then filled with, pumpkin chips, will be found very nice.

Musk-melon chips may be done in the same manner.

TO PRESERVE PINE-APPLES.

Take fine large pine-apples; pare them, and cut off a small round piece from the bottom, of each; let the freshest and. best of the top leaves remain on. Have ready on a slow fire, a large preserving kettle with a thin syrup barely sufficient to cover the fruit. In making this syrup allow a pound of fine loaf-sugar to every quart of water, and half the white of a beaten egg; all to be mixed before it goes on the fire. Then boil and skim it, and when the scum ceases to rise, put in the pine-apples, and simmer them slowly an hour. Then take them out to cool, cover them carefully and pat them away till next day; saving the syrup in another vessel. Next day, put them into the same syrup, and simmer them again an hour. On the third day, repeat the process. The fourth day, make a strong fresh syrup, allowing but a pint of water to each pound of sugar, and to every three pounds the beaten white of one egg. When this syrup has boiled, and is completely skimmed, put in the pine-apples, and simmer them half an hour. Then take them out to cool, and set them aside till next morning. Boil them again, half an hour in the same syrup, and repeat this for seven or eight days, or till you can pierce through the pine-apple with a straw from a corn-broom. At the last of these boilings enrich the syrup by allowing to each pound of sugar a quarter of a pound more; and, having boiled and skimmed it, put in the pine apples for half an hour. Then take them out, and when quite cold put each into a separate glass jar, and fill up with the syrup.

Pine apples may be preserved in slices by a very simple process. Pare them, and cut them into round pieces near an inch thick, and take out the core from the centre of each slice. Allow a pound of loaf-sugar to every pound of the sliced pine-apple. Powder the sugar, and strew it in layers between the slices of pine-apple. Cover it and let it set all night. Next morning measure some clear spring or pump water, allowing half a pint to each pound of sugar. Beat some white of egg, (one white to four pounds of sugar,) and when it is a very stiff froth, stir it gradually into the water. Then mix with it the pine-apple and sugar, and put the whole into a preserving kettle. Boil and skim it well, till the pine-apple is tender and bright all through. Then take it out, and when cold, put it up in wide-mouthed glass jars, or in large tumblers.

TO PREPARE FRESH PINE-APPLES.

Cut off the top and bottom and pare off the rind. Then cut the pine-apples in round slices half an inch thick, and put them into a deep dish, sprinkling every slice with powdered loaf-sugar. Cover them, and let them lie in the sugar for an hour or two, before they are to be eaten.

PRESERVED LEMONS.

Take large fine ripe lemons, that have no blemishes. Choose those with thin, smooth rinds. With a sharp, knife scoop a hole in the stalk end of each, large enough to admit the handle of a tea-spoon. This hole is to enable the syrup to penetrate the inside of the lemons. Put them into a preserving kettle with clear water, and boil them gently till you find them tender, keeping the kettle uncovered. Then take them oat, drain, and cool them, and put them into a small tub. Prepare a thin syrup of a pound of loaf-sugar to a quart of water. When you have boiled and skimmed it, pour it over the lemons and cover them. Let them stand in the syrup till next day. Then poor the syrup from the lemons, and spread them on a large dish. Boil it a quarter of an hour, and pour it over them again, having first returned them to the tub. Cover them, and let them again stand till next day, when you must again boil the syrup and pour it over them. Repeat this process every day till you find that the lemons are quite clear, and that the syrup has penetrated them thoroughly. If you find the syrup becoming too weak, add a little more sugar to it. Finally, make a strong syrup in the proportion of half a pint of water to a pound of sugar, adding a jill of raw lemon-juice squeezed from fresh lemons, and allowing to every four pounds of sugar the beaten white of an egg. Mix all well together in the kettle. Boil and skim it, and when the scum ceases to rise, pour the syrup boiling hot over the lemons; and covering them closely, let them stand undisturbed for four days. Then look at them, and if you find that they have not sucked in enough of the syrup to make the inside very sweet, boil them gently in the syrup for a quarter of an hour. When they are cold, put them up in glass jars.

You may green lemons by burying them in a kettle of vine leaves when you give them the first boiling in the clear water.

Limes may be preserved by this receipt; also oranges.

To prepare fresh oranges for eating, peel and cut them in round slices and remove the seeds. Strew powdered loaf-sugar over them. Cover them and let them stand an hour before they are eaten.

ORANGE MARMALADE.

Take fine large ripe oranges, with thin deep-coloured skins. Weigh them, and allow to each pound of oranges a pound of loaf-sugar. Pare off the yellow outside of the rind from half the oranges as thin as possible; and putting it into a pan with plenty of cold water, cover it closely (placing a double cloth beneath the tin cover) to keep in the steam, and boil it slowly till it is so soft that the head of a pin will pierce it. In the mean time grate the rind from the remaining oranges, and put it aside; quarter the oranges, and take out all the pulp and the juice; removing the seeds and core. Put the sugar into a preserving kettle, with a half pint of clear water to each pound, and mix it with some beaten white of egg, allowing one white of egg, to every four pounds of sugar. When the sugar is all dissolved, put it on the fire, and boil and skim it till it is quite clear and thick. Next take the boiled parings, and cut them into very small pieces, not more than, half an inch long; put them into the sugar, and boil them in it ten minutes. Then put in the pulp and juice of the oranges, and the grated rind, (which will much improve the colour,) and boil all together for about twenty minutes, till it is a transparent mass. When cold, pot it up in glass jars, laying brandy paper on the top.

Lemon marmalade may be made in a similar manner, but you must allow a pound and a half of sugar to each pound of lemons.

ORANGE JELLY.

Take fourteen large ripe oranges, and grate the yellow rind from seven of them. Dissolve an ounce of isinglass in as much warm water as will cover it. Mix the juice with a pound of loaf-sugar broken up, and add the grated, rind and the isinglass. Put it into a porcelain pan over hot coals and stir it till it boils. Then, skim it well. Boil it ten minutes, and strain it (but do not squeeze it) through a jelly-bag till it is quite clear. Put it into a mould to congeal, and when you want to turn it out dip the mould into lukewarm water. Or you may put it into glasses at once.

You must have a pint of juice to a pound of sugar.

A few grains of saffron boiled with the jelly will improve the colour without affecting the taste.

PRESERVED PEACHES.

Take large juicy ripe peaches; free-stones are the best, as they have a finer flavour than the cling-stones, and are much more manageable both to preserve, and to eat. Pare them, and cut them in half, or in quarters, leaving out the stones, the half of which you must save. To every pound of the peaches allow a pound of loaf-sugar. Powder the sugar, and strew it among your peaches. Cover them and let them stand all night. Crack half the peach-stones, break them up, put them into a small sauce-pan and boil them slowly in as much water as will cover them. Then when the water is well flavoured with the peach-kernels, strain them out, and set the water aside. Take care not to use too much of the kernel-water; a very little will suffice. Put the peaches into a preserving kettle, and boil them in their juice over a quick fire; (adding the kernel-water,) and skimming them all the time. When they are quite clear, which should be in half an hour, take them off, and put them into a tureen. Boil the syrup five minutes longer, and pour it hot over the peaches. When they are cool, put them into glass jars, and tie them up with paper dipped in brandy laid next to them.

Apricots, nectarines, and large plums maybe preserved in the same manner.

PEACHES FOR COMMON USE.

Take ripe free-stone peaches; pare, stone, and quarter them. To six pounds of the cut peaches allow three pounds of the best brown sugar. Strew the sugar among the peaches, and set them away. Next morning add a handful of peach leaves, put the whole into a preserving kettle, and boil it slowly about an hour and three quarters, or two hours, skimming it well. When cold, put it up in jars and keep it for pies, or for any common purpose.

BRANDY PEACHES.

Take large white or yellow free-stone peaches, the finest you can procure. They must not be too ripe. Rub off the down with a flannel, score them down the seam with a large needle, and prick every peach to the stone in several places. Scald them with boiling water, and let them remain in the water till it becomes cold, keeping them well covered. Repeat the scalding three times: it is to make them white. Then wipe them, and spread them on a soft table-cloth, covering them over with several folds. Let them remain in the cloth to dry. Afterwards put them into a tureen, or a large jar, and pour on as much white French brandy as will cover them well. Carefully keep the air from them, and let them remain in the brandy for a week. Then make a syrup in the usual manner, allowing to each pound of peaches a pound of loaf-sugar and half a pint of water mixed with a very little beaten white of egg; one white to three or four pounds of sugar.

When the syrup has boiled, and been well skimmed, put in the peaches and boil them slowly till they look clear; but do not keep them boiling more than half an hour. Then take them out, drain them, and put them into large glass jars. Mix the syrup, when it is cold, with the brandy in which you had the peaches, and pour it over them. Instead of scalding the peaches to whiten them, you may lay them for an hour in sufficient cold weak lye to cover them well. Turn them frequently while in the lye, and wipe them dry afterwards.

Pears and apricots may be preserved in brandy, according to the above receipt. The skin of the pears should he taken off, but the stems left on.

Large egg plums may be preserved in the same manner.

Another way of preparing brandy peaches is, after rubbing off the down and pricking them, to put them into a preserving kettle with cold water, and simmer them slowly till they become hot all through; but they must not be allowed to boil. Then dry them in a cloth, and let them lie till they are cold, covering them closely from the air. Dissolve loaf-sugar in the best white brandy, (a pound of sugar to a quart of brandy,) and having put the peaches into large glass jars, pour the brandy and sugar over them (without boiling) and cover the jars well with leather.

Pears, apricots, and egg plums may also be done in this manner.

PEACH MARMALADE.

Take ripe yellow free-stone peaches; pare, stone, and quarter them. To each pound of peaches, allow three quarters of a pound of powdered loaf-sugar, and half an ounce of bitter almonds, or peach-kernels blanched in scalding water, and pounded smooth in a mortar. Scald the peaches in a very little water, mash them to a pulp, mix them with the sugar and pounded-almonds, and put the whole into a preserving kettle. Let it boil to a smooth thick jam, skimming and stirring it well, and keeping the pan covered as much as possible. Fifteen minutes will generally suffice for boiling it. When cold, put it up in glass jars.

Plum marmalade may be made in this manner, flavouring it with pounded plum-kernels.

PEACH JELLY.

Take fine juicy free-stone peaches and pare and quarter them. Scald them in a very little water, drain and mash them, and squeeze the juice through a jelly-bag. To every pint of juice allow a pound of loaf-sugar, and a few of the peach-kernels. Having broken up the kernels and boiled them by themselves for a quarter of an hour in just as much water as will cover them, strain off the kernel-water, and add it to the juice. Mix the juice with the sugar, and when it is melted, boil them together fifteen minutes, till it becomes a thick jelly. Skim it well when it boils. Try the jelly by taking a little in a spoon and holding it in the open air to see if it congeals. If you find, that after sufficient boiling, it still continues thin, you can make it congeal by stirring in an ounce or more of isinglass, dissolved and strained. When the jelly is done, put it into tumblers, and lay on the top double tissue paper cut exactly to fit the inside of the glass; pressing it down with your fingers.

You may make plum jelly in the same manner, allowing a pound and a half of sugar to a pint of juice.

TO PRESERVE APRICOTS.

Take ripe apricots; scald them, peel them, cut them in half, and extract the stones. Then weigh the apricots, and to each pound allow a pound of loaf-sugar. Put them into a tureen or large pan, in alternate layers of apricots and sugar; cover them, and let them stand all night. Next morning put all together into a preserving kettle, and boil them moderately a quarter of an hour. Then take them out, spread them on dishes, and let them stand till next day. Then boil them again in the same syrup another quarter of an hour. Afterwards, spread them out to cool, put them into glass jars, and pour the syrup over them. Peaches may be preserved in the same manner. Also large plums or green gages; but to the plums you must allow additional sugar.

TO DRY PEACHES.

The best peaches for drying are juicy free-stones. They must be quite ripe. Cut them in half, and take out the stones. It is best not to pare them; as dried peaches are much richer with the skin on, and it dissolves and becomes imperceptible when they are cooked. Spread them out in a sunny balcony or on a scaffold, and let them dry gradually till they become somewhat like leather; always bringing them in at sunset, and not putting them out if the weather is damp or cloudy. They may also be dried in kilns or large ovens.

Apples are dried in the same manner, except that they must be pared and quartered.

Cherries also may be dried in the sun, first taking out all the stones. None but the largest and best cherries should be used for drying.

TO PRESERVE QUINCES.

Take large, yellow, ripe quinces, and having washed and wiped them, pare them and extract the cores. Quarter the quinces, or cut them into round slices an inch thick, and lay them in scalding water (closely covered) for an hour, or till they are tender. This will prevent them from hardening, Put the parings, cores, and seeds into a preserving kettle, cover them with the water in which you coddled the quinces, and boil them an hour, keeping them closely covered all the time. To every pint of this liquor allow a pound of loaf-sugar; and having dissolved the sugar in it, put it over the fire in the preserving kettle. Boil it up and skim it, and when the scum has ceased rising, put in the quinces, and boil them till they are red, tender, and clear all through, but not till they break. Keep the kettle closely covered while the quinces are in it, if you wish to have them bright coloured. You may improve the colour by boiling with them a little cochineal sifted through a muslin rag.

When they are done, take them out, spread them on large dishes to cool, and then put them into glasses. Give the syrup another boil up, and it will be like a fine jelly. Pour it hot over the quinces, and when cold, tie up the jars with brandy paper.

TO PRESERVE QUINCES WHOLE.

Take those that are large, smooth, and yellow; pare them and extract the cores, carefully removing all the blemishes. Boil the quinces in a close kettle with the cores and parings, in sufficient water to cover them. In half an hour take, them out, spread them to cool, and add to the cores and parings some small inferior quinces cut in quarters, but not pared or cored; and pour in some more water, just enough to boil them. Cover the pan, and let them simmer for an hour. Then take it off, strain the liquid, measure it, and to each quart allow a pound of loaf-sugar. Put the sugar to melt in the liquid, and let it set all night. Next day boil the quinces in it for a quarter of an hour, and then take them out and cool them, saving the syrup. On the following day repeat the same; and the fourth day add a quarter of a pound more sugar to each pint of the syrup, and boil the quinces in it twelve minutes. If by this time they are not tender, bright, and transparent all through, repeat the boiling.

When they are quite done, put quince jelly or marmalade into the holes from whence you took the cores; put the quinces into glass jars and pour the syrup over them. If convenient, it is a very nice way to put up each quince in a separate tumbler.

QUINCE JELLY.

Take fine ripe yellow quinces, wash them and remove all the blemishes, cut them in pieces, but do not pare or core them. Put them into a preserving-pan with clear spring water. If you, are obliged to use river water, filter it first; allowing one pint to twelve large quinces. Boil them gently till they are all soft and broken. Then put them into a jelly-bag, and do not squeeze it till after the clear liquid has ceased running. Of this you must make the *best* jelly, allowing to each pint a pound of loaf-sugar. Having dissolved the sugar in the liquid, boil them together about twenty minutes, or till you have a thick jelly.

In the meantime, squeeze out all that is left in the bag. It will not be clear, but you can make of it a very good jelly for common purposes.

QUINCE MARMALADE.

Take six pounds of ripe yellow quinces; and having washed them clean, pare and core them, and cut them into small pieces. To each pound of the cut quinces allow half a pound of powdered loaf-sugar. Put the parings and cores into a kettle with water enough to cover them, and boil them slowly till they are all to pieces, and quite soft. Then having put the quinces with the sugar into a porcelain preserving kettle, strain over them, through a cloth, the liquid from the parings and cores. Add a little cochineal powdered, and sifted through thin muslin. Boil the whole over a quick fire till it becomes a thick smooth mass, keeping it covered except when you are skimming it; and always after skimming, stir it up well from the bottom.

When cold, put it up in glass jars. If you wish to use it soon, put it warm into moulds, and when if is cold, set the moulds in lukewarm water, and the marmalade will turn out easily.

QUINCE CHEESE.

Have fine ripe quinces, and pare and core them. Cut them into pieces, and weigh them; and to each pound of the cut quinces, allow half a pound of the best brown sugar. Pat the cores and parings into a kettle, with water enough to cover them, keeping the lid of the kettle closed. When you find that they are all boiled to pieces and quite soft, strain off the water over the sugar, and when it is entirely dissolved, put it over the fire and boil it to a thick syrup, skimming it well. When no more scum rises, put in the quinces, cover them closely, and boil them all day over a slow fire, stirring them and mashing them down with a spoon till they are a thick smooth paste. Then take it out, and put it into buttered tin pans or deep dishes. Let it set to get cold. It will then turn out so firm that you may cut it into slices like cheese. Keep it in a dry place in broad stone pots. It is intended for the tea-table.

PRESERVED APPLES.

Take fine ripe pippin or bell-flower apples. Pare and core them, and either leave them whole, or cut them into quarters. Weigh them, and to each pound of apples allow a pound of loaf-sugar. Put the apples into a stew-pan with just water enough to cover them, and let them boil slowly for about half an hour. They must be only parboiled. Then strain the apple water over the sugar into a preserving kettle, and when the sugar is melted put it on the fire with the yellow rind of some lemons pared thin, allowing four lemons lo a dozen apples. Boil the syrup till clear and thick, skimming; it carefully; then put in the apples, and after they have boiled slowly a quarter of an hour, add the juice of the lemons. Let it boil about fifteen minutes longer, or till the apples are tender and clear, but not till they break. When they are cold, put them into jars, and covering them closely, let them set a week. At the end of that time give them another boil in the same syrup; apples being more difficult to keep than any other fruit.

You may colour them red by adding, when you boil them in the syrup, a little cochineal.

BAKED APPLES.

Take a dozen fine large juicy apples, and pare and core them; but do not cut them in pieces. Put them side by side into a large baking-pan, and fill up with brown sugar the holes from whence you have extracted the cores. Pour into each a little lemon-juice, or a few drops of essence of lemon, and stick in every one a long piece of lemon-peel evenly cut. Into the bottom of the pan put a very little water, just enough to prevent the apples from burning. Bake them about an hour, or till they are tender all through, but not till they break. When, done, set them away to get cold.

If closely covered they will keep, two days. They may be eaten at tea with cream. Or at dinner with a boiled custard poured over them. Or you may cover them with, sweetened cream flavored with a little essence of lemon, and whipped to a froth. Heap the froth over every apple so as to conceal them entirely.

APPLE JELLY.

Take twenty large ripe juicy pippins. Pare, core, and chop them to pieces. Put them into a jar with the yellow rind of four lemons, pared thin and cut into little bits Cover the jar closely, and set it into a pot of hot water Keep the water boiling hard all round it till the apples are dissolved, Then strain them through a jelly-bag, and mix with the liquid the juice of the lemons. To each pint of the. mixed juice allow a pound of loaf-sugar. Put them into a porcelain kettle, and when the sugar is melted, set it on the fire, and boil and skim it for about twenty minutes, or till it becomes a thick jelly. Put it into tumblers, and cover it with double tissue paper nicely fitted to the inside of the top. The red or Siberian crab apple makes a delicious jelly, prepared in the above manner.

APPLE BUTTER.

This is a compound of apples and cider boiled together till of the consistence of soft butter. It is a very good article on the tea-table, or at luncheon. It can only be made of sweet new cider fresh from the press, and not yet fermented.

Fill a very large kettle with cider, and boil it till reduced to one half the original quantity. Then have ready some fine juicy apples, pared, cored, and quartered; and put as many into the kettle as can be kept moist by the cider. Stir it frequently, and when the apples are stewed quite soft, take them out with a skimmer that has holes in it, and put them into a tub. Then add more apples to the cider, and stew them soft in the same manner, stirring them nearly all the time with a stick. Have at hand some more cider ready boiled, to thin the apple butter in case you should find it too thick in the kettle.

If you make a large quantity, (and it is not worth while to prepare apple butter on a small scale,) it will take a day to stew the apples. At night leave them to cool in the tubs, (which must be covered with cloths,) and finish next day by boiling the apple and cider again till the consistence is that of soft marmalade, and the colour a very dark brown.

Twenty minutes or half an hour before you finally take it from the fire, add powdered cinnamon, cloves, and nutmeg to your taste. If the spice is boiled too long, it will lose its flavour.

When it is cold, put it into stone jars, and cover it closely. If it has been well made, and sufficiently boiled, it will keep a year or more.

It must not he boiled in a brass or bell-metal kettle, on account of the verdigris which the acid will collect in it, and which will render the apple butter extremely unwholesome, not to say, poisonous.

TO PRESERVE GREEN CRAB APPLES.

Having washed your crab apples, (which should be full grown,) cover the bottom and sides of your preserving kettle with vine leaves, and put them in; spreading a thick layer of vine leaves over them. Fill up the kettle with cold, water, and hang it over a slow fire early in the morning; simmer them slowly, but do not allow them to boil. When they are quite yellow, take them out, peel off the skin with a penknife, and extract the cores very neatly.. Put them again into the kettle with fresh vine leaves and fresh water, and hang them again over a slow fire to simmer, but not to boil. When they have remained long enough in the second vine leaves to become green, take them out, weigh them, and allow a pound and a half of loaf-sugar to each pound of crab apples. Then after the kettle has been well washed and wiped, put them into it with a thick layer of sugar between each layer of apples, and about half a pint of water, for each pound and a half of sugar. You may add the juice and yellow peel of some lemons. Boil them gently till they are quite clear and tender throughout. Skim them well, and keep the kettle covered when you are not skimming. When done, spread them on large dishes to cool, and then tie them up in glass jars with brandy papers.

TO PRESERVE RED CRAB APPLES.

Take red or Siberian crab apples when they are quite ripe and the seeds are black. Wash and wipe them, and put them into a kettle with sufficient water to cover them. Simmer them very slowly till you find that the skin will come off easily. Then take them out and peel and core them; extract the cores carefully with a small knife, so as not to break the apples. Then weigh them, and to every pound of crab apples allow a pound and a half of loaf-sugar and a half pint of water. Put the sugar and water into a preserving kettle, and when they are melted together, set it over the fire and let it boil. After skimming it once, put in the crab apples, adding a little cochineal powder rubbed with a knife into a very small quantity of white brandy till it has dissolved. This will greatly improve the colour of the apples. Cover them and let them boil till clear and tender, skimming the syrup when necessary. Then spread them out on dishes, and when they are cold, put them into glass jars and pour the syrup over them.

The flavour will be greatly improved by boiling with them in the syrup, a due proportion of lemon-juice and the peel of the lemons pared thin so as to have the yellow part only. If you use lemon-juice put a smaller quantity of water to the sugar. Allow one large lemon or two smaller ones to each pound of crab apples.

If you find that after they have been kept awhile, the syrup inclines to become dry or candied, give it another boil with the crab apples in it, adding a tea-cup full of water to about three or four pounds of the sweetmeat.

TO PRESERVE GREEN GAGES.

Take large fine green gages that are not perfectly ripe. Weigh them, and to each pound of fruit allow a pound and a half of loaf-sugar. Put a layer of fresh vine leaves at the bottom of a porcelain preserving kettle, place on it a layer of gages, then cover them with a layer of vine leaves, and so on alternately, finishing with a layer of leaves at the top. Fill up the kettle with hard water, and set it over a slow fire. When the gages rise to the top, take them out and peel them, putting them on a sieve as you do so. Then replace them in the kettle with fresh vine leaves and water; cover them very closely, so that no steam can escape, and hang them up at some distance above the fire to green slowly for six hours. They should be warm all the time, but must not boil. When they are a fine green, take them carefully out, spread them on a hair sieve to drain, and make a syrup of the sugar, allowing a half pint of water to each pound and a half of sugar. When it has boiled and been skimmed, put in the green gages and boil them gently for a quarter of an hour. Then take them out and spread them to cool. Next day boil them in the same syrup for another quarter of an hour. When cold, put them into glass jars with the syrup, and tie them up with brandy paper.

To preserve them whole without peeling, you must prick each at the top and bottom, with a large needle.

TO PRESERVE PLUMS.

Take fine ripe plums; weigh them, and to each pound allow a pound and a half of loaf-sugar. Put them into a pan, and scald them in boiling water to make the skins come off easily. Peel them, and throw them as you do so into a large china pitcher. Let them set for an hour or two, and then take them out, saving all the juice that has exuded from them while in the pitcher. Spread the plums out on large dishes, and cover them with half the sugar you have allotted to them, (it must be previously powdered,) and let them lie in it all night. Next morning pour the juice out of the pitcher into a porcelain preserving kettle, add the last half of the sugar to it, and let it melt over the fire. When it has boiled skim it, and then put in the plums. Boil them over a moderate fire, for about half an hour. Then take them out one by one with a spoon, and spread them on large dishes to cool. If the syrup is not sufficiently thick and clear, boil and skim it a little longer till it is. Put the plums into glass jars and pour the syrup warm over them.

The flavour will be much improved by boiling in the syrup with the fruit a handful or more of the kernels of plums, blanched in scalding water and broken in half. Take the kernels out of the syrup before you pour it into the jars.

You may preserve plums whole, without peeling, by pricking them deeply at each end with a large needle.

Green gages and damsons maybe preserved according to this receipt.

PLUMS FOR COMMON USE.

Take fine ripe plums, and cut them in half. Extract all the stones, and spread out the plums on large dishes. Set the dishes on the sunny roof of a porch or shed, and let the plums have the full benefit of the sun for three or four days, taking them in, as soon as it is off, or if the sky becomes cloudy. This will half dry them. Then pack them closely in stone jars with a thick layer of the best brown sugar between every layer of plums; putting plenty of sugar at the bottom and top of the jars. Cover them closely, and set them away in a dry place.

If they have been properly managed, they will keep a year; and are very good for pies and other purposes, in the winter and spring.

Peaches may be prepared for keeping in the same manner.

EGG PLUMS WHOLE.

Take large egg plums that are not quite ripe, and prick them all over with a small silver fork. Leave on the stems. To three pounds of plums allow three pounds and a half of loaf-sugar, broken small or powdered. Put the plums and sugar into a preserving kettle, and pour in one half pint of clear hard water. Hang the kettle over a moderate fire, and boil and skim it, As soon as the skin begins to crack or shrivel, take out the plums one at a time, (leaving the syrup on the fire,) and spread them on large dishes to cool. Place them in the open air, and as soon as they are cool enough to be touched with your fingers, smooth the skin down where it is broken or ruffled, When quite cold, return them to the syrup, (which in the mean time must have been kept slowly simmering,) and boil the plums again till they are quite clear, but not till they break. Put them warm into large glass or queen's-ware jars, and pour the syrup over them.

TO PRESERVE PEARS.

Take large fine juicy pears that are not perfectly ripe, and pare them smoothly and thin; leaving on the stems, but cutting out the black top at the blossom end of the fruit. As you pare them, lay them in a pan of cold water. Make a thin syrup, allowing a quart of water to a pound of loaf-sugar. Simmer the pears in it for about half an hour. Then pat them into a tureen, and let them lie in the syrup for two days, There must be syrup enough to cover them well. After two days, drain the syrup front the pears, and add to it more sugar, in the proportion of a pound to each pint of the thin syrup. Stir in a very little beaten white of egg, (not more than one white to three or four pounds of sugar,) add some fresh lemon-peel pared thin, and set the syrup over a brisk fire. Boil it for ten minutes and skim it well. Then acd sufficient lemon-juice to flavour it; and put in the pears. Simmer them in the strong syrup till they are quite transparent. Then take them out, spread them to cool, and stick a clove in the blossom end of each. Put them into glass jars; and having kept the syrup warm over the fire while the pears were tooling, pour it over them.

If you wish to have them red, add a little powdered cochineal to the strong syrup when you put in your pears.

BAKED PEARS.

The best for baking are the large late ones, commonly called pound pears. Pare them, cut them in half, and take out the cores. Lay them in a deep white dish, with a thin slip of fresh lemon-peel in the place from which each core was taken. Sprinkle them with sugar, and strew some whole cloves or some powdered cinnamon-among them. Pour into the dish some port wine. To a dozen large pears you may allow half a pound of sugar, and a pint of wine. Cover the dish, with a large sheet of brown paper tied on; set it in a moderate oven, and let them bake till tender all through which you may ascertain by sticking a broom twig through them. They will he done in about an hour, or they may probably require more time; but you must not let them remain long enough in the oven, to break or fall to pieces. When cool, put them up in a stone jar. In cold weather they will keep a week.

To bake smaller pears, pare them, but leave on the stems, and do not core them. Put them into a deep dish with fresh lemon, or orange-peel; throw on them some brown sugar or molasses; pour in at the bottom a little water to keep them from burning; and bake them till tender throughout.

TO PRESERVE GOOSEBERRIES.

The best way of preserving gooseberries is with jelly. They should be full grown but green. Take six quarts of gooseberries, and select three quarts of the largest and finest to preserve whole, reserving the others for the jelly. Put the whole ones into a pan with sufficient water to cover them, and simmer them slowly till they begin to be tender; but do not keep them on the fire till they are likely to burst. Take them out carefully with a perforated skimmer to drain the warm water from them, and lay them directly in a pan of cold water. Put those that you intend for the jelly into a stew-pan, allowing to each quart of gooseberries half a pint of water. Boil them fast till they go all to pieces, and stir and mash them with a spoon. Then put them into a jelly-bag that has been first dipped in hot water, and squeeze through it all the juice. Measure the juice, and to each pint allow a pound and a half of loaf-sugar. Break up the sugar, and put it into a preserving kettle; pour the juice over it, and let it stand to melt, stirring it frequently. When it has all dissolved, set it over the fire, put the gooseberries into it, and let them boil twenty minutes, or till they are quite clear, and till the jelly is thick and congeals in the spoon when you hold it in the air. If the gooseberries seem likely to break, take them out carefully, and let the jelly boil by itself till it is finished. When all is done, put up the gooseberries and the jelly together in glass jars.

Strawberries, raspberries, grapes, currants or any small fruit may in a similar manner be preserved in jelly.

TO STEW GOOSEBERRIES.

Top and tail them. Pour some boiling water on the gooseberries, cover them up, and let them set about half an hour, or till the skin is quite tender, but not till it bursts, as that will make the juice run out into the water. Then pour off the water, and mix with the gooseberries an equal quantity of sugar. Put them into a porcelain stew-pan or skillet, and set it on hot coals, or on a charcoal furnace. In a few minutes you may begin to mash them against the side of the pan with a wooden spoon. Let them stew about half an hour, stirring them frequently. They must be quite cold before they are used for any thing.

GOOSEBERRY FOOL.

Having stewed two quarts of gooseberries in the above manner, stir them as soon as they are cold into a quart of rich boiling milk. Grate in a nutmeg, and covering the pan, let the gooseberries simmer in the milk for five minutes. Then stir in the beaten yolks of two or three eggs, and immediately remove it from the fire. Keep on the cover a few minutes longer; then turn out the mixture into a deep dish or a glass bowl, and set it away to get cold, before it goes to table. Eat it with sponge-cake. It will probably require additional sugar.

Gooseberries prepared in this manner make a very good pudding, with the addition of a little grated bread. Use both whites and yolks of the eggs. Stir the mixture well, and bake it in a deep dish. Eat it cold, with sugar grated over it.

TO BOTTLE GOOSEBERRIES.

For this purpose the gooseberries must be large and full grown, but quite green. Top and tail them, and put them into wide-mouthed bottles as far up as the beginning of the neck. Cover the bottom of a large boiler or kettle with saw-dust or straw. Stand the bottles of gooseberries (slightly corked) upright in the boiler, and pour round them cold water to each, as far up as the fruit. Put a brisk fire under the boiler, and when the water boils up, instantly take out the bottles and fill them up to the mouth with boiling water, which you must have ready in a tea-kettle. Cork them again slightly, and when quite cold put in the corks very tight and seal them. Lay the bottles on their sides in a box of dry sand, and turn them every day for four or five weeks. If properly managed, the gooseberries will keep a year, and may be used at any time, by stewing them with sugar.

You may bottle damsons in the same manner; also grapes.

PRESERVED RASPBERRIES.

Take a quantity of ripe raspberries, and set aside the half, selecting for that purpose the largest and firmest. Then put the remainder into your preserving pan, mash them, and set them over the fire. As soon as they have come to a boil, take them out, let them cool, and then squeeze them through a bag.

While they are cooling, prepare your sugar, which must be fine loaf. Allow a pound of sugar to every quart of whole raspberries. Having washed the kettle clean, put the sugar into it, allowing half a pint of cold water to two pounds of sugar. When it has melted in the water, put it on the fire, and boil it till the scum ceases to rise, and it is a thick syrup; taking care to skim it well. Then put in the whole raspberries, and boil them rapidly a few minutes, but not long enough to cause them to burst. Take them out with a skimmer full of holes, and spread them on a large dish to cool. Then mix with the syrup the juice of those you boiled first, and let it boil about ten or fifteen minutes. Lastly, put in the whole fruit, and give it one more boil, seeing that it does not break.

Put it warm into glass jars or tumblers, and when quite cold cover it closely with paper dipped in brandy, tying another paper tightly over it.

Strawberries may be done in the same manner; blackberries also.

RASPBERRY JAM.

Take fine raspberries that are perfectly ripe. Weigh them, and to each pound of fruit allow three quarters of a pound of fine loaf-sugar. Mash the raspberries, and break up the sugar. Then mix them together, and put them into a preserving kettle over a good fire. Stir them frequently and skim them. The jam will be done in half an hour. Put it warm into glasses, and lay on the top a white paper cut exactly to fit the inside, and dipped in brandy. Then tie on another cover of very thick white paper.

Make blackberry jam in the same manner.

TO PRESERVE CRANBERRIES.

The cranberries must be large and ripe. Wash them, and to six quarts of cranberries allow nine pounds of the best brown sugar. Take three quarts of the cranberries, and put them into a stew-pan with a pint and a half of water. Cover the pan, and boil or stew them, till they are all to pieces. Then squeeze the juice through a jelly-bag. Put the sugar into a preserving kettle, pour the cranberry juice over it and let it stand till it is all melted, stirring it up frequently. Then place the kettle over the fire, and put in the remaining three quarts of whole cranberries. Let them boil till they are tender, clear, and of a bright colour, skimming them frequently. When done, put them, warm into jars with the syrup, which should be like a thick jelly.

RED CURRANT JELLY.

The currants should be perfectly ripe and gathered on a dry day. Strip them from the stalks, and put them into a stone jar. Cover the jar, and set it up to the neck in a kettle of boiling water. Keep the water boiling round the jar till the currants are all broken, stirring them up occasionally. Then put them into a jelly-bag, and squeeze out all the juice. To each pint of juice allow a pound and a quarter of the best loaf-sugar. Put the sugar into a porcelain kettle, pour the juice over it, and stir it frequently till it is all melted. Then set the kettle over a moderate fire, and let it boil twenty minutes, or till you find that the jelly congeals in the spoon when, you hold it in the air; skim it carefully all the time. When the jelly is done, pour it warm into tumblers, and cover each with two rounds of white tissue paper, cut to fit exactly the inside of the glass.

Jelly of gooseberries, plums, raspberries, strawberries, barberries, blackberries, grapes, and other small fruit may all be made in this manner.

WHITE CURRANT JELLY.

The currants should be quite ripe, and gathered on a dry day. Having stripped them from the stalks, put them into a close stone jar, and set it in a kettle of boiling water. As soon as the currants begin to break, take them out and strain them through a linen cloth. To each pint of juice allow a pound and a quarter of the best double refined loaf-sugar; break it small, and put it into a porcelain preserving pan with barely sufficient water to melt it; not quite half a pint to a pound and a quarter of sugar; it must be either clear spring water or river water filtered. Stir up the sugar while it is dissolving, and when all is melted, put it over a brisk fire, and boil and skim it till clear and thick. When the scum ceases to rise, put in the white currant juice and boil it fast for ten minutes. Then put it warm into tumblers, and when it is cold, cover it with double white tissue paper.

In making this jelly, use only a silver spoon, and carefully observe all the above precautions, that it may be transparent and delicate. If it is not quite clear and bright when done boiling, you may run it again through a jelly-bag.

White raspberry jelly may be prepared in the same manner. A very nice sweetmeat is made of white raspberries preserved whole, by putting them in white currant jelly during the ten minutes that you are boiling the juice with the syrup. You may also preserve red raspberries whole, by boiling them in red currant jelly.

BLACK CURRANT JELLY.

Take large ripe black currants; strip them from the stalks, and mash them with the back of a ladle. Then put them into a preserving kettle with a tumbler of water to each quart of currants; cover it closely, set it over a moderate fire, and when the currants have come to a boil, take them out, and squeeze them through a jelly-bag. To each pint of juice you may allow about a pound of loaf-sugar, and (having washed the preserving kettle perfectly clean) put in the sugar with the juice; stir them together till well mixed and dissolved, and then boil it not longer than ten minutes; as the juice of black currants being very thick will come to a jelly very soon, and if boiled too long will be tough and ropy.

Black currant jelly is excellent for sore throats; and if eaten freely on the first symptoms of the disease, will frequently check, it without any other remedy. It would be well for all families to keep it in the house.

GRAPE JELLY.

Take ripe juicy grapes, pick them from the steins; put them into a large earthen pan, and mash them with the back of a wooden ladle, or with a potato beetle. Put them into a kettle, (without any water,) cover them, closely, and let them boil for a quarter of an hour; stirring them up occasionally from the bottom. Then squeeze them through a jelly-bag, and to each pint of juice allow a pound of loaf-sugar. Dissolve the sugar in the grape juice; then put it over a quick fire in a preserving kettle, and boil and skim it twenty minutes. When it is a clear thick jelly, take it off, put it warm into tumblers, and cover them with double tissue paper cut to fit the inside.

In the same manner you may make an excellent jelly for common use, of ripe fox grapes and the best brown sugar; mixing with the sugar before it goes on the fire, a little beaten white of egg; allowing two whites to three pounds of sugar.

GRAPES.

Take some large close bunches of fine grapes, (they must not be too ripe,) and allow to each bunch a quarter of a pound of bruised sugar candy. Put the grapes and the sugar candy into large jars, (about two-thirds full,) and fill them up with French brandy. Tie them up closely, and keep them in a dry place. Morella cherries may be done in the same manner.

Foreign grapes are kept in bunches, laid lightly in earthen jars of dry saw-dust.

TO KEEP WILD GRAPES.

Gather the small black wild grapes late in the season, after they have been ripened by a frost. Pick them from the stems, and put them into stone jars, (two-thirds full,) with layers of brown sugar, and fill them up with cold molasses. They will keep all winter; and they make good common pies. If they incline to ferment in the jars, give them a bail with additional sugar.

TO PRESERVE STRAWBERRIES.

Strawberries for preserving should be large and ripe. They will keep best if gathered in dry weather, when there has been no rain for at least two days. Having hulled, or topped and tailed them all, select the largest and firmest, and spread them out separately on flat dishes; having first weighed them, and allowed to each pound of strawberries a pound of powdered loaf-sugar. Sift half the sugar over them. Then take the inferior strawberries that were left, and those that, are over ripe; mix with them an equal quantity of powdered sugar, and mash them. Put them into a basin covered with a plate, and set them over the fire in a pan of boiling water, till they become a thick juice; then strain it through a bag and mix with it the other half of the sugar that you have allotted to the strawberries, which are to be done whole. Put it into a porcelain kettle, and boil and skim it till the scum ceases to rise; then put in the whole strawberries with the sugar in which they have been lying, and all the juice that may have exuded from them. Set them over the fire in the syrup, just long enough to heat them a little; and in a few minutes take them out, one by one, with a tea-spoon, and spread them on dishes to cool; not allowing them to touch each other. Then take off what scum may arise from the additional sugar. Repeat this several times, taking out the strawberries and cooling them till they become quite clear. They must not be allowed to boil; and if they seem likely to break, they should be instantly and finally taken from the fire. When quite cold, put them with the syrup into tumblers, or into white queen's-ware pots. If intended to keep a long time it will be well to put at the top a layer of apple jelly.

TO PRESERVE CHERRIES.

Take large ripe morella cherries; weigh them, and to each pound allow a pound of loaf-sugar. Stone the cherries, (opening them with a sharp quill,) and save the juice that comes from them in the process. As you stone them, throw them into a large pan or tureen, and strew about half the sugar over them, and let them lie in it an hour or two after they are all stoned. Then put them into a preserving kettle with the remainder of the sugar, and boil and skim them till the fruit is clear and the syrup thick.

CHERRIES PRESERVED WHOLE.

The large carnation cherries are the best for this purpose. They should be quite ripe. Prick every one in several places with a needle, and leave on the stalks cut short. To each pound of cherries allow a pound and a quarter of the best loaf-sugar. Spread them on large dishes, and strew over them a thick layer of the sugar powdered fine; about a quarter of a pound of sugar to each pound of cherries. Or you may put them into a large tureen, and disperse the sugar among them, cover them, and let them set all night. In the morning get some ripe red currants; pick them, from the stalks, and squeeze them through a linen cloth till you have just sufficient juice to moisten the remaining sugar, which you must have ready in a preserving kettle. When the sugar has melted in the currant juice, put it over the fire, and when it has been well boiled and skimmed, put in the cherries and simmer them half an hour, or till they are so clear that you can see the stones through them. Then take them up one at a time, and spread them out to cool. Taste one, and if the sugar does not seem, to have sufficiently penetrated it, return them to the syrup and boil them a little longer, but do not allow them to break. If you are willing to take the trouble, you may put them out to cool three or four times while simmering. This will make them more transparent, and prevent them from bursting.

CHERRY JELLY.

Take fine juicy red cherries, and stone them. Save half the stones, crack them, and extract the kernels. Put the cherries and the kernels into a preserving kettle over a slow fire, and let them boil gently in their juice for half an hour. Then transfer them to a jelly-bag, and squeeze out the juice. Measure it, and to each pint allow a pound of fine loaf-sugar. Dissolve the sugar in the juice, and then boil and skim it for twenty or thirty minutes. Put it up in tumblers covered with tissue paper.

CHERRY JAM.

To each pound of cherries allow three quarters of a pound of the best brown sugar. Stone them, and as you do so throw the sugar gradually into the pan with them. Cover them and let them set all night. Next day, boil them slowly till the cherries and sugar form a thick smooth mass. Put it up in queen's-ware jars.

TO DRY CHERRIES.

Choose the finest and largest red cherries for this purpose. Store them, and spread them on large dishes in the sun, till they become quite dry, taking them in as soon as the sun is off, or if the sky becomes cloudy. Put them up in stone jars, strewing among them some of the best brown sugar.

The common practice of drying cherries with the stones in, (to save trouble,) renders them so inconvenient to eat, that they are of little use, when done in that manner.

With the stones extracted, dried cherries will be found very good for common pies.

BARBERRY JELLY.

Take ripe barberries, and having stripped them from the stalks, mash them, and boil them in their juice for a quarter of an hour. Then squeeze them through a bag: allow to each pint of juice, a pound of loaf-sugar; and having melted the sugar in the juice, boil them together twenty or twenty-five minutes, skimming carefully. Put it up in tumblers with tissue paper.

FROSTED FRUIT.

Take large ripe cherries, plums, apricots, or grapes, and cut off half the stalk. Have ready in one dish some beaten white of egg, and in another some fine loaf-sugar, powdered and sifted. Dip the fruit first into the white of egg, and then roll it one by one in the powdered sugar. Lay a sheet of white paper on the bottom of a reversed sieve, set it on a stove or in some other warm place, and spread the fruit on the paper till the icing is hardened.

PEACH LEATHER.

To six pounds of ripe peaches, (pared and quartered,) allow three pounds of the best brown sugar. Mix them together, and put them, into a preserving kettle, with barely water enough to keep them from burning. Pound and mash them a while with a wooden beetle. Then boil and skim them for three hours or more, stirring them nearly all the time. When done, spread them thinly on large dishes, and set them in the sun for three or four days; Finish the drying by loosening the peach leather on the dishes, and setting them in the oven after the bread is taken out, letting them remain till the oven is cold. Roll up the peach leather and put it away in a box.

Apple leather may be made in the same manner.

RHUBARB JAM.

Peel the rhubarb stalks and cut them into small square pieces. Then weigh them, and to each pound allow three quarters of a pound of powdered loaf-sugar. Put the sugar and the rhubarb into a large, deep, white pan, in alternate layers, the top layer to be of sugar—cover it, and let it stand all night. In the morning, put it into a preserving kettle, and boil it slowly till the whole is dissolved into a thick mass, stirring it frequently, and skimming it before every stirring. Put it warm into glass jars, and tie it up with brandy paper.

PASTRY, PUDDINGS, ETC.

THE BEST PLAIN PASTE.

All paste should be made in a very cool place, as heat renders it heavy. It is far more difficult to get it light in summer than in winter. A marble slab is much better to roll it on than a paste-board. It will be improved in lightness by washing the butter in very cold water, and squeezing and pressing out all the salt, as salt is injurious to paste. In New York and in the Eastern states, it is customary, in the dairies, to put more salt in what is called fresh butter, than in New Jersey, Pennsylvania, and Delaware. This butter, therefore, should always undergo the process of washing and squeezing before it is used for pastry or cakes. None but the very best butter should be taken for those purposes; as any unpleasant taste is always increased by baking. Potted butter never makes good paste. As pastry is by no means an article of absolute necessity, it is better not to have it at all, than to make it badly, and of inferior ingredients; few things being more unwholesome than hard, heavy dough. The flour for paste should always be superfine.

You may bake paste in deep dishes or in soup plates. For shells that are to be baked empty, and afterwards filled with stewed fruit or sweetmeats, deep plates of block tin with broad edges are best. If you use patty-pans, the more flat they are the better. Paste always rises higher and is more perfectly light and flaky, when unconfined at the sides while baking. That it may be easily taken out, the dishes or tins should be well buttered.

To make a nice plain paste,—sift three pints of superfine flour, by rubbing it through a sieve into a deep pan. Divide a pound of fresh butter into four quarters. Cut up one quarter into the flour, and rub it fine with your hands. Mix in, gradually, as much cold water as will make a tolerably stiff dough, and then knead it slightly. Use as little water as possible or the paste will be tough. Sprinkle a little flour on your paste-board, lay the lump of dough upon it, and knead it a very short time. Flour it, and roll it out into a very thin sheet, always rolling from you. Flour your rolling-pin to prevent its sticking. Take a second quarter of the butter, and with your thumb, spread it all over the sheet of paste. If your hand is warm, use a knife instead of your thumb; for if the butter oils, the paste will be heavy. When you have put on the layer of butter, sprinkle it with a very little flour, and with your hands roll up the paste as you would a sheet of paper. Then flatten it with a rolling-pin, and roll it out a second time into a thin sheet. Cover it with another layer of butter, as before, and again roll it up into a scroll. Flatten it again, put on the last layer of butter, flour it slightly, and again roll up the sheet. Then cut the scroll into as many pieces as you want sheets for your dishes or patty-pans. Roll out each piece almost an inch thick. Flour your dishes, lay the paste lightly on them, notch the edges, and bake it a light brown. The oven must be moderate. If it is too hot, the paste will bake before it has risen sufficiently. If too cold, it will scarcely rise at all, and will be white and clammy. When you begin to make paste in this manner, do not quit it till it is ready for the oven. It must always be baked in a close oven where no air can reach it.

The best rolling-pins, are those that are straight, and as thick at the ends as in the middle. They should be held by the handles, and the longer the handles the more convenient. The common rolling-pins that decrease in size towards the ends, are much less effective, and more tedious, as they can roll so little at a time; the extremities not pressing on the dough at all.

All, pastry is best when fresh. After the first day it loses much of its lightness, and is therefore more unwholesome.

COMMON PIE CRUST.

Sift two quarts of superfine flour into a pan. Divide one pound of fresh butter into two equal parts, and cut up one half in the flour, rubbing it fine. Mix it with a very little cold water, and make it into a round lump. Knead it a little. Then flour your paste-board, and roll the dough out into a large thin sheet. Spread it all over with the remainder of the butter. Flour it, fold it up, and roll it out again. Then fold it again, or roll it into a scroll. Cut it into as many pieces as you want sheets of paste, and roll each not quite an inch thick. Butter your pie-dish.

This paste will do for family use, when covered pies are wanted. Also for apple dumplings, pot-pies, &c.; though all boiled paste is best when made of suet instead of butter. Short cakes may be made of this, cut out with the edge of a tumbler. It should always be eaten fresh.

SUET PASTE.

Having removed the skirt and stringy fibres from a pound of beef suet, chop it as fine as possible. Sift two quarts of flour into a deep pan, and rub into it one half of the suet. Make, it into a round lump of dough, with cold water, and then knead it a little. Lay the dough on your paste-board, roll it out very thin, and cover it with the remaining half of the suet. Flour it, roll it out thin again, and then roll it into a scroll. Cut it into as many pieces as you want sheets of paste, and roll them out half an inch thick.

Suet paste should always be boiled. It is good for plain puddings that are made of apples, gooseberries, blackberries or other fruit; and for dumplings. If you use it for pot-pie, roll it the last time rather thicker than if wanted for any other purpose. If properly made, it will be light and flaky, and the suet imperceptible. If the suet is minced very fine, and thoroughly incorporated with the flour, not the slightest lump will appear when the paste comes to table.

The suet must not be melted before it is used; but merely minced as fine as possible and mixed cold with the flour.

If for dumplings to eat with boiled mutton, the dough must be rolled out thick, and cut out of the size you want them, with a tin, or with the edge of a cup or tumbler.

DRIPPING PASTE.

To a pound of fresh beef-dripping, that has been nicely clarified, allow two pounds and a quarter of flour. Put the flour into a large pan, and mix the dripping with it, rubbing it into the flour with your hands till it is thoroughly incorporated. Then make it into a stiff dough with a little cold water, and roll it out twice. This may be used for common meat pies.

LARD PASTE.

Lard for paste should never be used without an equal quantity of butter. Take half a pound of nice lard, and half a pound of fresh butter; rub them together into two pounds and a quarter of flour, and mix it with a little cold water to a stiff dough. Roll it out twice. Use it for common pies. Lard should always be kept in tin.

POTATO PASTE.

To two quarts of flour, allow fourteen good sized potatoes. Boil the potatoes till they are thoroughly done throughout. Then peel, and mash them very fine. Rub them through a cullender.

Having sifted the flour into a pan, add the potatoes gradually; rubbing them well into the flour with your hands. Mix in sufficient cold water to make a stiff dough. Roll it out evenly, and you may use it for apple dumplings, boiled apple pudding, beef-steak pudding, &c.

Potato paste must be sent to table quite hot; as soon as it cools it becomes tough and heavy. It is unfit for baking; and even when boiled is less light than suet paste.

FINE PUFF PASTE.

To every pound of the best fresh butter allow a pound or a quart of superfine flour. Sift the flour into a deep pan, and then sift on a plate some additional flour to use for sprinkling and rolling. Wash the butter through two cold waters; squeezing out all the salt, and whatever milk may remain in it; and then make it up with your hands into a round lump, and put it in ice till you are ready to use it. Then divide the butter into four equal parts. Cut up one of the quarters into the pan of flour; and divide the remaining three quarters into six pieces, [Footnote: Or into nine; and roll it in that number of times.] cutting each quarter in half. Mix with a knife the flour and butter that is in the pan, adding by degrees a very little cold water till you have made it into a lump of stiff dough. Then sprinkle some flour on the paste-board, (you should have a marble slab,) take the dough from the pan by lifting it out with the knife, lay it on the board, and flouring your rolling-pin, roll out the paste into a large thin sheet. Then with the knife, put all over it, at equal distances, one of the six pieces of butter divided into small bits. Fold up the sheet of paste, flour it, roll it out again, and add in the same manner another of the portions of butter. Repeat this process till the butter is all in. Then fold it once more, lay it on a plate, and set it in a cool place till you are ready to use it. Then divide it into as many pieces as you want sheets of paste; roll out each sheet, and put them into buttered plates or patty-pans. In using the rolling-pin, observe always to roll from you. Bake the paste in a moderate oven, but rather quick than slow. No air must be admitted to it while baking.

The edges of paste should always be notched before it goes into the oven. For this purpose, use a sharp penknife, dipping it frequently in flour as it becomes sticky. The notches should be even and regular. If you do them imperfectly at first, they cannot be mended by sticking on additional bits of paste; as, when baked, every patch will be doubly conspicuous. There are various ways of notching; one of the neatest is to fold over one corner of each notch; or you may arrange the notches to stand upright and lie flat, alternately, all round the edge. They should be made small and regular. You may form the edge into leaves with the little tin cutters made for the purpose.

If the above directions for puff paste are carefully followed, and if it is not spoiled in baking, it will rise to a great thickness and appear in flakes or leaves according to the number of times you have put in the butter.

It should be eaten the day it is baked.

SWEET PASTE.

Sift a pound and a quarter of the finest flour, and three ounces of powdered loaf-sugar into a deep dish. Cut up in it ten ounces of the best fresh butter and rub it fine with your hands. Make a hole in the middle, pour in the yolks of two beaten eggs, and mix them with the flour, &c. Then wet the whole to a stiff paste with half a pint of rich milk. Knead it well, and roll it out.

This paste is intended for tarts of the finest sweetmeats. If used as shells they should be baked empty, and filled when cool. If made into covered tarts they may be iced all over, in the manner of cakes, with beaten white of egg and powdered loaf-sugar. To make puffs of it, roll it out and cut it into round pieces with the edge of a large tumbler, or with a tin cutter. Lay the sweetmeat on one half of the paste, fold the other over it in the form of a half-moon, and unite the edges by notching them together. Bake them in a brisk oven, and when cool, send them to table handsomely arranged, several on a dish.

Sweet paste is rarely used except for very handsome entertainments. You may add some rose water in mixing it.

SHELLS.

Shells of paste are made of one sheet each, rolled out in a circular form, and spread over the bottom, sides, and edges of buttered dishes or patty-pans, and baked empty; to be filled, when cool, with stewed fruit, (which for this purpose should be always cold,) or with sweetmeats. They should be made either of fine puff paste, or of the best plain paste, or of sweet paste. They are generally rolled out rather thick, and will require about half an hour to bake. The oven should be rather quick, and of equal heat throughout; if hotter in one part than in another, the paste will draw to one side, and be warped and disfigured. The shells should be baked of a light brown. When cool, they must be taken out of the dishes on which they were baked, and transferred to plates and filled with the fruit.

Shells of puff paste will rise best if baked on flat patty-pans, or tin plates. When they are cool, pile the sweetmeats on them in a heap.

The thicker and higher the paste rises, and the more it flakes in layers or leaves, the finer it is considered.

Baking paste as empty shells, prevents it from being moist or clammy at the bottom.

Tarts are small shells with fruit in them.

PIES.

Pies may be made with any sort of paste. It is a fault to roll it out too thin; for if it has not sufficient substance, it will, when baked, be dry and tasteless. For a pie, divide the paste into two sheets; spread one of them over the bottom and sides of a deep dish well buttered. Next put in the fruit or other ingredients, (heaping it higher in the centre,) and then place the other sheet of paste on the top as a lid or cover; pressing the edges closely down, and afterwards crimping or notching them with a sharp small knife.

In making pies of juicy fruit, it is well to put on the centre of the under crust a common tea-cup, laying the fruit round it and over it. The juice will collect under the cup, and not be liable to run out from between the edges.

There should be plenty of sugar strewed among the fruit as you put it into the pie.

Preserves should never be put into covered pies. The proper way is to lay them in baked shells.

All pies are best the day they are baked. If kept twenty-four hours the paste falls and becomes comparatively hard, heavy, and unwholesome. If the fruit is not ripe, it should be stewed with sugar, and then allowed to get cold before it is put into the pie. If put in warm it will make the paste heavy. With fruit pies always have a sugar dish on the table, in case they should not be found sweet enough.

STANDING PIES.

Cut up half a pound of butter, and put it into a sauce-pan with three quarters of a pint of water; cover it, and set it on hot coals. Have ready in a pan two pounds of sifted flour; make a hole in the middle of it, pour in the melted butter as soon as it boils, and then with a spoon gradually mix in the flour. When it is well mixed, knead it with your hands into a stiff dough. Sprinkle your paste-board with flour, lay the dough upon it, and continue to knead it with your hands till it no longer sticks to them, and is quite light. Then let it stand an hour to cool. Cut off pieces for the bottom and top; roll them out thick, and roll out a long piece for the sides or walls of the pie, which you must fix on the bottom so as to stand up all round; cement them together with white of egg, pinching and closing them firmly. Then put in the ingredients of your pie, (which should be venison, game, or poultry,) and lay on the lid or top crust, pinching the edges closely together. You may ornament the sides and top with leaves or flowers of paste, shaped with a tin cutter, and notch or scollop the edges handsomely. Before you set it in the oven glaze it all over with white of egg. Bake it four hours. These pies are always eaten cold, and in winter will keep two or three weeks, if the air is carefully excluded from them; and they may be carried to a considerable distance.

A PYRAMID OF TARTS.

Roll out a sufficient quantity of the best puff paste, or sugar paste; and with oval or circular cutters, cut it out into seven or eight pieces of different sizes; stamping the middle of each with the cutter you intend using for the next. Bake them all separately, and when they are cool, place them on a dish in a pyramid, (gradually diminishing in size,) the largest piece at the bottom, and the smallest at the top. Take various preserved fruits, and lay some of the largest on the lower piece of paste; on the next place fruit that is rather smaller; and so on till you finish at the top with the smallest sweetmeats you have. The upper one may be not so large as a half-dollar, containing only a single raspberry or strawberry.

Notch all the edges handsomely. You may ornament the top or pinnacle of the pyramid with a sprig of orange blossom or myrtle.

APPLE AND OTHER PIES.

Take fine juicy acid apples; pare, core, and cut them into small pieces. Have ready a deep dish that has been lined with paste. Fill it with the apples; strewing among them layers of brown sugar, and adding the rind of a lemon pared thin, and also the juice squeezed in, or some essence of lemon. Put on another sheet of paste as a lid; close the edges well, and notch them. Bake the pie in a moderate oven, about three quarters of an hour. Eat it with cream and sugar, or with cold boiled custard.

If the pie is made of early green apples, they should first be stewed with a very little water and plenty of brown sugar.

What are called sweet apples are entirely unfit for cooking, as they become tough and tasteless; and it is almost impossible to get them sufficiently done.

When you put stewed apples into baked shells, grate nutmeg over the top. You may cover them with cream whipped to a stiff froth, and heaped on them.

Cranberries and gooseberries should be stewed with sugar before they are put into paste. Peaches should be cut in half or quartered, and the stones taken out. The stones of cherries and plums should also be extracted.

Raspberries or strawberries, mixed with cream and white sugar, may he put raw into baked shells.

RHUBARB TARTS.

Take the young green stalks of the rhubarb plant, or spring fruit as it is called in England; and having peeled off the thin skin, cut the stalks into small pieces about an inch long, and put them into a sauce-pan with plenty of brown sugar, and its own juice. Cover it, and let it stew slowly till it is soft enough to mash to a marmalade. Then set it away to cool. Have ready some fresh baked shells; fill them with the stewed rhubarb, and grate white sugar over the top.

For covered pies, cut the rhubarb very small; mix a great deal of sugar with it, and put it in raw. Bake the pies about three quarters of an hour.

MINCE PIES.

These pies are always made with covers, and should be eaten warm. If baked the day before, heat them on the stove or before the fire.

Mince-meat made early in the winter, and packed closely in stone jars, will keep till spring, if it has a sufficiency of spice and liquor. Whenever you take out any for use, pour some additional brandy into the jar before you cover it again, and add some more sugar. No mince-meat, however, will keep well unless all the ingredients are of the best quality. The meat should always be boiled the day before you want to chop it.

GOOD MINCE-MEAT.

Take a bullock's heart and boil it, or two pounds of the lean of fresh beef. When it is quite cold, chop it very fine. Chop three pounds of beef suet (first removing the skin and strings) and six pounds of large juicy apples that have been pared and cored. Then, stone six pounds of the best raisins, (or take sultana raisins that are without stones,) and chop them also. Wash and dry three pounds of currants. Mix all together; adding to them the grated peel and the juice of two or three large oranges, two table-spoonfuls of powdered cinnamon, two powdered nutmegs, and three dozen powdered cloves, a tea-spoonful of beaten mace, one pound of fine brown sugar, one quart of Madeira wine, one pint of French brandy, and half a pound of citron cut into large slips. Having thoroughly mixed the whole, put it into a stone jar, and tie it up with brandy paper.

THE BEST MINCE-MEAT,

Take a large fresh tongue, rub it with a mixture, in equal proportions, of salt, brown sugar, and powdered cloves. Cover it, and let it lie two days, or at least twenty-four hours. Then boil it two hours, and when, it is cold, skin it, and mince it very fine. Chop also three pounds of beef suet, six pounds of sultana raisins, and six pounds of the best pippin apples that have been previously pared and cored. Add three pounds of currants, picked, washed and dried; two large table-spoonfuls of powdered cinnamon; the juice and grated rinds of four large lemons; one pound of sweet almonds, one ounce of bitter almonds, blanched and pounded in a mortar with half a pint of rose water; also four powdered nutmegs; two dozen beaten cloves; and a dozen blades of mace powdered. Add a pound of powdered white sugar, and a pound of citron cut into slips. Mix all together, and moisten it with a quart of Madeira, and a pint of brandy. Put it up closely in a stone jar with brandy paper; and when you take any out, add some more sugar and brandy.

Bake this mince-meat in puff paste.

You may reserve the citron to put in when you make the pies. Do not cut the slips too small, or the taste will be almost imperceptible.

VERY PLAIN MINCE-MEAT.

Take a piece of fresh beef, consisting of about two pounds of lean, and one pound of fat. Boil it, and when it is quite cold, chop it fine. Or you may substitute cold roast beef. Pare and core some fine juicy apples, cut them in pieces, weigh three pounds, and chop them. Stone four pounds of raisins, and chop them also. Add a large table-spoonful of powdered cloves, and the same quantity of powdered cinnamon. Also a pound of brown sugar. Mix all thoroughly, moistening it with a quart of bottled or sweet cider. You may add the grated peel and the juice of an orange.

Bake it in good common paste.

This mince-meat will do very well for children or for family use, but is too plain to be set before a guest. Neither will it keep so long as that which is richer and more highly seasoned. It is best to make no more of it at once than you have immediate occasion for.

MINCE-MEAT FOR LENT.

Boil a dozen eggs quite hard, and chop the yolks very fine. Chop also a dozen pippins, and two pounds of sultana raisins. Add two pounds of currants, a pound of sugar, a table-spoonful of powdered cinnamon, a tea-spoonful of beaten mace, three powdered nutmegs, the juice and grated peel of three large lemons, and half a pound of citron cut in large strips. Mix these ingredients thoroughly, and moisten the whole with a pint of white wine, half a pint of rose-water, and half a pint of brandy. Bake it in very nice paste.

These mince pies may be eaten by persons who refrain from meat in Lent.

ORANGE PUDDING.

Grate the yellow part of the rind, and squeeze the juice of two large, smooth, deep-coloured oranges. Stir together to a cream, half a pound of butter, and half a pound of powdered white sugar, and add a wine-glass of mixed wine and brandy. Beat very light six eggs, and stir them gradually into the mixture. Put it into a buttered dish with a broad edge, round which lay a border of puff-paste neatly notched. Bake it half an hour, and when cool grate white sugar over it.

You may add to the mixture a Naples biscuit, or two finger biscuits, grated.

LEMON PUDDING.

May be made precisely in the same manner as the above; substituting lemons for oranges.

QUINCE PUDDING.

Take six large ripe quinces; pare them, and cut out all the blemishes. Then scrape them to a pulp, and mix the pulp with half a pint of cream, and half a pound of powdered sugar, stirring them together very hard. Beat the yolks of seven eggs, (omitting all the whites except two,) and stir them gradually into the mixture, adding two wine glasses of rose water. Stir the whole well together and bake it in a buttered dish three quarters of an hour Grate sugar over it when cold.

If you cannot obtain cream, you may substitute a quarter of a pound of fresh butter stirred with the sugar and quince. A baked apple pudding may be made in the same manner.

ALMOND PUDDING.

Take half a pound of shelled sweet almonds, and three ounces of shelled bitter almonds, or peach-kernels. Scald and peel them; throwing them, as they are peeled, into cold water. Then pound them one at a time in a marble mortar, adding to each a few drops of rose water; otherwise they will be heavy and oily. Mix the sweet and bitter almonds together by pounding them alternately; and as you do them, take them out and lay them on a plate. They must each be beaten to a fine smooth paste, free from the smallest lumps. It is best to prepare them the day before you make the pudding.

Stir to a cream half a pound of fresh butter and half a pound of powdered white sugar; and by degrees pour into it a glass of mixed wine and brandy. Beat to a stiff froth, the whites only, of twelve eggs, (you may reserve the yolks for custards or other purposes,) and stir alternately into the butter and sugar the pounded almonds and the beaten white of egg. When the whole is well mixed, put it into a buttered dish and lay puff paste round the edge. Bake it about half an hour, and when cold grate sugar over it.

ANOTHER ALMOND PUDDING.

Blanch three quarters of a pound of shelled sweet almonds, and three ounces of shelled bitter almonds, and beat them in a mortar to a fine paste; mixing them well, and adding by degrees a tea-cup full, or more, of rose water. Boil in a pint of rich milk, a few sticks of cinnamon broken up, and a few blades of mace. When the milk has come to a boil, take it off the fire, strain it into a pan, and soak in it five stale rusks cut into slices. They must soak till quite dissolved. Stir to a cream three quarters of a pound of fresh butter, mixed with the same quantity of powdered loaf-sugar. Beat ten eggs very light, yolks and whites together, and then stir alternately into the butter and sugar, the rusk, eggs, and almonds. Set it on a stove or a chafing dish, and stir the whole together till very smooth and thick. Put it into a buttered dish and bake it three quarters of an hour. It must be eaten cool or cold.

COCOA-NUT PUDDING.

Having opened a cocoa-nut, pare off the brown skin from the pieces, and wash them all in cold water. Then weigh three quarters of a pound, and grate it into a dish. Cut up half a pound of butter into half a pound of powdered loaf-sugar, and stir them together to a cream; add to them a glass of wine and rose water mixed. Beat the whites only, of twelve eggs, till they stand alone on the rods; and then stir the grated cocoa-nut and the beaten white of egg alternately into the butter and sugar; giving the whole a hard stirring at the last. Put the mixture into a buttered dish, lay puff paste round the flat edge, and bake it half an hour in a moderate oven. When cool, grate powdered sugar over it.

ANOTHER COCOA-NUT PUDDING.

Peel and cut up the cocoa-nut, and wash, and wipe the pieces. Weigh one pound, and grate it fine. Then, mix with it three stale rusks or small sponge-cakes, grated also. Stir together till very light half a pound of butter and half a pound of powdered white sugar, and add a glass of white wine. Beat six whole eggs very light, and stir them gradually into the butter and sugar in turn with the grated cocoa-nut. Having stirred the whole very hard at the last, put it into a buttered dish and bake it half an hour.

PUMPKIN PUDDING.

Take a pint of pumpkin that has been stewed soft, and pressed through a cullender. Melt in half a pint of warm milk, a quarter of a pound of butter, and the same quantity of sugar, stirring them well together. If you can conveniently procure a pint of rich cream it will be better than the milk and butter. Beat eight eggs very light, and add them gradually to the other ingredients, alternately with the pumpkin. Then stir in a wine glass of rose water and two glasses of wine mixed together; a large tea-spoonful of powdered mace and cinnamon mixed, and a grated nutmeg. Having stirred the whole very hard, put it into a buttered dish and bake it three quarters of an hour.

A SQUASH PUDDING.

Pare, cut in pieces, and stew in a very little water, a yellow winter squash. When it is quite soft, drain it dry, and mash it in a cullender. Then put it into a pan, and mix with it a quarter of a pound of butter. Prepare two pounded crackers, or an equal quantity of grated stale bread. Stir gradually a quarter of a pound of powdered sugar into a quart of rich milk, and add by degrees, the squash, and the powdered biscuit. Beat nine eggs very light, and stir them gradually into the mixture. Add a glass of white wine, a glass of brandy, a glass of rose water, and a table-spoonful of mixed spice, nutmeg, mace, and cinnamon powdered. Stir the whole very hard, till all the ingredients are thoroughly mixed. Bake it three quarters of an hour in a buttered dish; and when cold, grate white sugar over it.

YAM PUDDING.

Take one pound of roasted yam, and rub it through a cullender. Mix with it half a pound of white sugar, a pint of cream or half a pound of butter, a tea-spoonful of powdered cinnamon, a grated nutmeg, and a wine glass of rose water, and one of wine. Set it away to get cold. Then beat six eggs very light. Stir them into the mixture. Put it into a buttered dish and bake it half an hour. Grate sugar over it when cold.

CHESTNUT PUDDING,

May be made in the above manner.

POTATO PUDDING.

Boil a pound of fine potatoes, peel them, mash them, and rub them through a cullender. Stir together to a cream, three quarters of a pound of sugar and the same quantity of butter. Add to them gradually, a wine glass of rose water, a glass of wine, and a glass of brandy; a tea-spoonful of powdered mace and cinnamon, a grated nutmeg, and the juice and grated peel of a large lemon. Then beat six eggs very light, and add them by degrees to the mixture, alternately with the potato. Bake it three quarters of an hour in a buttered dish.

SWEET POTATO PUDDING.

Take half a pound of sweet potatoes, wash them, and put them into a pot with a very little water, barely enough to keep them from burning. Let them simmer slowly for about half an hour; they must be only parboiled, otherwise they will be soft, and may make the pudding heavy. When they are half done, take them out, peel them, and when cold, grate them. Stir together to a cream, half a pound of butter and a quarter of a pound and two ounces of powdered sugar, add a grated nutmeg, a large tea-spoonful of powdered cinnamon, and half a tea-spoonful of beaten mace. Also the juice and grated peel of a lemon, a wine glass of rose water, a glass of wine, and a glass of brandy. Stir these ingredients well together. Beat eight eggs very light, and stir them into the mixture in turn with the sweet potato, a little at a time of each. Having stirred the whole very hard at the last, put it into a buttered dish and bake it three quarters of an hour.

CARROT PUDDING.

May be made in the above manner.

GREEN CORN PUDDING.

Take twelve ears of green corn, as it is called, (that is, Indian corn when full grown, but before it begins to harden and turn yellow,) and grate it. Have ready a quart of rich milk, and stir into it by degrees a quarter of a pound of fresh butter, and a quarter of a pound of sugar. Beat four eggs till quite light; and then stir them into the milk, &c. alternately with the grated corn, a little of each at a time. Put the mixture into a large buttered dish, and bake it four hours. It may be eaten either warm or cold, For sauce, beat together butter and white sugar in equal proportions, mixed with grated nutmeg.

To make this pudding—you may, if more convenient, boil the corn and cut it from the cob; but let it get quite cold before you stir it into the milk. If the corn has been previously boiled, the pudding will require but two hours to bake.

SAGO PUDDING.

Pick, wash, and dry half a pound of currants; and prepare a tea-spoonful of powdered cinnamon; a half tea-spoonful of powdered mace; and a beaten nutmeg. Have ready six table-spoonfuls of sago, picked clean, and soaked for two hours in cold water. Boil the sago in a quart of milk till quite soft. Then stir alternately into the milk, a quarter of a pound of butter, and six ounces of powdered sugar, and set it away to cool. Bent eight eggs, and when they are quite light, stir them gradually into the milk, sago, &c. Add the spice, and lastly the currants; having dredged them well with flour to prevent their sinking. Stir the whole very hard, put it into a buttered dish, and bake it three quarters of an hour. Eat it cold.

ARROW ROOT PUDDING.

Take four tea-cups full of arrow root, and dissolve it in a pint of cold milk. Then boil another pint of milk with some broken cinnamon, and a few bitter almonds or peach-leaves. When done, strain it hot over the dissolved arrow root; stir it to a thick smooth batter, and set it away to get cold. Next, beat six eggs very light, and stir them into the batter, alternately with a quarter of a pound of powdered white sugar. Add a grated nutmeg and some fresh lemon-peel grated. Put the mixture into a buttered dish, and bake it an hour. When cold, cut some slices of preserved quince or peach, and arrange them handsomely all over the top of the pudding; or ornament it with strawberries, or raspberries preserved whole.

GROUND RICE PUDDING.

Mix a quarter of a pound of ground rice with a pint of cold milk, till it is a smooth batter and free from lumps. Boil three pints of milk; and when it has boiled, stir in gradually the rice batter, alternately with a quarter of a pound of butter. Keep it over the fire, stirring all the time, till the whole is well mixed, and has boiled hard. Then take it off, add a quarter of a pound of white sugar; stir it well, and set it away to cool. Beat eight eggs very light and stir them into the mixture when it is quite cold. Then strain it through a sieve, (this will make it more light and delicate,) add a grated nutmeg, and a large tea-spoonful of powdered cinnamon. Stir in the juice and the grated peel of a lemon, or a small tea-spoonful of essence of lemon. Put it into a deep dish or dishes, and bake it an hour. As soon as it comes out of the oven, lay slips of citron over the top; and when cold, strew powdered sugar on it.

A RICE PLUM PUDDING.

Take three jills of whole rice; wash it, and boil it in a pint of milk. When it is soft, mix in a quarter of a pound of butter, and set it aside to cool; and when it is quite cold, stir it into another pint of milk. Prepare a pound and a half of raisins or currants; if currants, wash and dry them; if raisins, seed them and cut them in half. Dredge them well with flour, to prevent their sinking; and prepare also a powdered nutmeg; a table-spoonful of mixed mace and cinnamon powdered; a wine glass of rose water; and a wine glass of brandy or white wine. Beat six eggs very light, and stir them into the mixture, alternately with a quarter of a pound of sugar. Then add by degrees the spice and the liquor, and lastly, stir in, a few at a time, the raisins or currants. Put the pudding into a buttered dish and bake it an hour and a half. Send it to table cool.

You may make this pudding of ground rice, using but half a pint instead of three jills.

A PLAIN RICE PUDDING.

Pick and wash a pint of rice, and boil it soft. Then drain off the water, and let the rice dry and get cold. Afterwards mix with it two ounces of butter, and four ounces of sugar, and stir it into a quart of rich milk. Beat four or five eggs very light, and add them gradually to the mixture. Stir in at the last a table-spoonful of mixed nutmeg and cinnamon. Bake it an hour in a deep dish.

A FARMER'S RICE PUDDING.

This pudding is made without eggs. Wash half a pint of rice through two cold waters, and drain it well. Stir it raw into a quart of rich milk, or of cream and milk mixed; adding a quarter of a pound of brown sugar, and a table-spoonful of powdered cinnamon. Put it into a deep pan, and bake it two hours or more. When done, the rice will be perfectly soft, which you may ascertain by dipping a tea-spoon into the edge of the pudding and taking out a little to try. Eat it cold.

RICE MILK.

Pick and wash half a pint of rice, and boil it in a quart of water till it is quite soft. Then drain it, and mix it with a quart of rich milk. You may add half a pound of whole raisins. Set it over hot coals, and stir it frequently till it boils. When it boils hard, stir in alternately two beaten eggs, and four large table-spoonfuls of brown sugar. Let it continue boiling five minutes longer; then take it off, and send it to table hot. If you put in raisins you must let it boil till they are quite soft.

A BOILED RICE PUDDING.

Mix a quarter of a pound of ground rice with a pint of milk, and simmer it over hot coals; stirring it all the time to prevent its being lumpy, or burning at the bottom. When it is thick and smooth, take it off, and pour it into an earthen pan. Mix a quarter of a pound of sugar, and a quarter of a pound of butter with half a pint of cream or very rich milk, and stir it into the rice; adding a powdered nutmeg, and the grated rind of two lemons, or half a tea-spoonful of strong oil of lemon. Beat the yolks of six eggs with the whites of two only. When the eggs are quite light, mix them gradually with the other ingredients, and stir the whole very hard. Butter a large bowl, or a pudding mould. Put in the mixture; tying a cloth tightly over the top, (so that no water can get in,) and boil it two hours. When done, turn it out into a dish. Send it to table warm, and eat it with sweetened cream, flavoured with a glass of brandy or white wine and a grated nutmeg.

A MARLBOROUGH PUDDING.

Pare, core and quarter six large ripe pippin apples. Stew them in half a pint of water. When they are soft but not broken, take them out, drain them through a sieve, and mash them to a paste with the back of a spoon. Mix with them six large table-spoonfuls of sugar and a quarter of a pound of butter, and set them away to get cold. Grate two milk biscuits or email sponge cakes, or an equal quantity of stale bread, and grate also the yellow peel, and squeeze the juice of a large lemon. Beat six eggs light, and when the apple is cold stir them gradually into it, adding the grated biscuit and the lemon. Stir in a wine glass of rose water and a grated nutmeg. Put the mixture into a buttered dish or dishes; lay round the edge a border of puff paste, and bake it three quarters of art hour. When cold, grate white sugar over the top, and ornament it with slips of citron handsomely arranged.

ALMOND CHEESE CAKE.

This though usually called a cheese cake, is in fact a pudding.

Cut a piece of rennet about two inches square, wash off the salt in cold water, and wipe it dry. Put it into a tea-cup, pour on it sufficient lukewarm water to cover it, and let it soak all night, or at least several hours. Take a quart of milk, which must be made warm, but not boiling. Stir the rennet-water into it. Cover it, and set it in a warm place. When the curd has become quite firm, and the whey looks greenish, drain off the whey, and set the curd in a cool place. While the milk is turning, prepare the other ingredients. Wash and dry half a pound of currants, and dredge them well with flour. Blanch three ounces of sweet and one ounce of bitter almonds, by scalding and peeling them. Then cool them in cold water, wiping them dry before you put them into the mortar. If you cannot procure bitter almonds, peach kernels may be substituted. Beat them, one at a time, in the mortar to a smooth paste, pouring in with every one a few drops of rose water to prevent their being oily, dull-coloured, and heavy. If you put a sufficiency of rose water, the pounded almond paste will be light, creamy, and perfectly white. Mix, as you do them, the sweet and bitter almonds together. Then beat the yolks of eight eggs, and when light, mix them gradually with the curd. Add five table-spoonfuls of cream, and a tea-spoonful of mixed spice. Lastly, stir in, by degrees, the pounded almonds, and the currants alternately. Stir the whole mixture very hard. Bake it in buttered dishes, laying puff paste round the edges. If accurately made, it will be found delicious. It must be put in the oven immediately.

COMMON CHEESE CAKE.

Boil a quart of rich milk. Beat eight eggs, put them to the milk, and let the milk and eggs boil together till they become a curd. Then drain it through a very clean sieve, till all the whey is out. Put the curd into a deep dish, and mix with it half a pound of butter, working them well together. When it is cold, add to it the beaten yolks of four eggs, and four large table-spoonfuls of powdered white sugar; also a grated nutmeg. Lastly, stir in, by degrees, half a pound of currants that have been previously picked, washed, dried, and dredged with flour. Lay. puff paste round the rim of the dish, and bake the cheese cake half an hour. Send it to table cold.

PRUNE PUDDING.

Scald a pound of prunes; cover them, and let them swell in the hot water till they are soft. Then drain them, and extract the stones; spread the prunes on a large dish, and dredge them with flour. Take one jill or eight large fable-spoonfuls from a quart of rich milk, and stir into it, gradually, eight spoonfuls of sifted flour. Mix it to a smooth batter, pressing out all the lumps with the back of the spoon. Beat six eggs very light, and stir them, by degrees, into the remainder of the milk, alternately with the batter that you have just mixed. Then add the prunes one at a time, stirring the whole very hard. Tie the pudding in a cloth that has been previously dipped in boiling water and then dredged with flour. Leave room for it to swell, but secure it firmly, so that no water can get in. Put it into a pot of boiling water, and boil it two hours. Send it to table hot, (not taking it out of the pot till a moment before it is wanted,) and eat it with cream sauce; or with butter, sugar, and nutmeg beaten together, and served up in a little tureen. A similar pudding may be made with whole raisins.

EVE'S PUDDING.

Pare, core, and quarter six large pippins, and chop them very fine. Grate stale bread till you have six ounces of crumbs, and roll fine six ounces of brown sugar. Pick, wash, and dry six ounces of currants, and sprinkle them with flour. Mix all these ingredients together in a large pan, adding six ounces of butter cut small, and two table-spoonfuls of flour. Beat six eggs very light, and moisten the mixture with them. Add a grated nutmeg, and a tea-spoonful of powdered cinnamon. Stir the whole very well together. Have ready a pot of boiling water. Dip your pudding cloth into it, shake it out, and dredge it with flour. Then put in the mixture, and tie it very firmly; leaving space for the pudding to swell, and stopping up the tying place with a paste of wetted flour. Boil it three hours; keeping at the fire a kettle of boiling water, to replenish the pot, that the pudding may be always well covered. Send it to table hot, and eat it with sweetened cream flavoured with wine and nutmeg.

CINDERELLAS OR GERMAN PUFFS.

Sift eight table-spoonfuls of the finest flour. Cut up in a quart of rich milk, half a pound of fresh butter, and set it on the stove, or near the fire, till it has melted. Beat eight eggs very light, and stir them gradually into the milk and butter, alternately with the flour. Add a powdered nutmeg, and a tea-spoonful of powdered cinnamon. Mix the whole very well to a fine smooth batter, in which there must be no lumps. Butter some large common tea-cups, and divide the mixture among them till they are half full or a little more. Set them immediately in a quick oven, and bake them about a quarter of an hour. When done, turn them out into a dish and grate white sugar over them. Serve them up hot, with a sauce of sweetened cream flavoured with wine and nutmeg; or you may eat them with molasses and butter; or with sugar and wine. Send them round whole, for they will fall almost as soon as cut.

A BOILED BREAD PUDDING.

Boil a quart of rich milk. While it is boiling, take a small loaf of baker's bread, such as is sold for five or six cents. It may be either fresh or stale. Pare off all the crust, and cut up the crumb into very small pieces. You should have baker's bread if you can procure it, as home-made bread may not make the pudding light enough. Put the bread into a pan; and when the milk boils, pour it scalding hot over the bread. Cover the pan closely, and let it steep in the hot steam for about three quarters of an hour. Then remove the cover, and allow the bread and milk to cool. In the mean time, beat four eggs till they are thick and smooth. Then beat into them a table-spoonful and a half of fine wheat flour. Next beat the egg and flour into the bread and milk, and continue to beat hard till the mixture is as light as possible; for on this the success of the pudding chiefly depends.

Have ready over the fire a pot of boiling water. Dip your pudding-cloth into it, and shake it out. Spread out the cloth in a deep dish or pan, and dredge it well with flour. Pour in the mixture, and tie up the cloth, leaving room for it to swell. Tie the string firmly and plaster up the opening (if there is any) with flour moistened with water. If any water gets into it the pudding will be spoiled.

See that the water boils when you put in the pudding, and keep it boiling hard. If the pot wants replenishing, do it with boiling water from a kettle. Should you put in cold water to supply the place of that which has boiled away, the pudding will chill, and become hard and heavy. Boil it an hour and a half.

Turn it out of the bag the minute before you send it to table. Eat it with wine sauce, or with sugar and butter, or molasses.

It will be much improved by adding to the mixture half a pound of whole raisins, well floured to prevent their sinking. Sultana raisins are best, as they have no seeds.

If these directions are exactly followed, this will be found a remarkably good and wholesome plain pudding.

For all boiled puddings, a square pudding-cloth which can be opened out, is much better than a bag. It should be very thick.

A BAKED BREAD PUDDING.

Take a stale five cent loaf of bread; cut off all the crust, and grate or rub the crumb as fine as possible. Boil a quart of rich milk, and pour it hot over the bread; then stir in a quarter of a pound of butter, and the same quantity of sugar, a glass of wine and brandy mixed, or a glass of rose water. Or you may omit the liquor and substitute the grated peel of a large lemon. Add a table-spoonful of raised cinnamon and nutmeg powdered. Stir the whole very well, cover it, and set it away for half an hour. Then let it cool. Beat seven or eight eggs very light, and stir them gradually into the mixture after it is cold. Then butter a deep dish, and bake the pudding an hour. Send it to table cool.

A BREAD AND BUTTER PUDDING.

Cut some slices of bread and butter moderately thick, omitting the crust; stale bread is best. Butter a deep dish, and cover the bottom with slices of the buttered bread. Have ready a pound of currants, picked, washed and dried. Spread one third of them thickly over the bread and butter, and strew on some brown sugar. Then put another layer of bread and butter, and cover it also with currants and sugar. Finish with a third layer of each, and pour over the whole four eggs, beaten very light and mixed with a pint of milk, and a wine glass of rose water. Bake the pudding an hour, and grate nutmeg over it when done. Eat it warm, but not hot.

You may substitute for the currants, raisins seeded, and cut in half.

This pudding may be made also with layers of stewed gooseberries instead of the currants, or with pippin apples pared, cored and minced fine.

A SUET PUDDING.

Mince very finely as much beef suet as will make two large table-spoonfuls. Grate two handfuls of bread-crumbs; boil a quart of milk and pour it hot on the bread. Cover it, and set it aside to steep for half an hour; then put it to cool. Beat eight eggs very light; stir the suet, and three table-spoonfuls of floor alternately into the bread and milk, and add, by degrees, the eggs. Lastly, stir in a table-spoonful of powdered nutmeg and cinnamon mixed, and a glass of mixed wine and brandy. Pour it into a bag that has been dipped in hot water and floured; tie it firmly, put it into a pot of boiling water, and boil it two hours. Do not take it up till immediately before it is wanted, and send it to table hot.

Eat it with wine sauce, or with molasses.

A CUSTARD PUDDING.

Take five table-spoonfuls out of a quart of cream or rich milk, and mix them with two large spoonfuls of fine flour. Set the rest of the milk to boil, flavouring it with half a dozen peach leaves, or with bitter almonds broken up. When it has boiled hard, take it off, strain it, and stir in the cold milk and flour. Set it away to cool, and beat very light ten yolks and four whites of eggs; add them to the milk, and stir in, at the last, a glass of brandy, or white wine, a powdered nutmeg, and a quarter of a pound of sugar. Butter a large bowl or mould; pour in the mixture; tie a cloth tightly over it; put it into a pot of boiling water, and boil it two hours, replenishing the pot with hot water from a tea-kettle. When the pudding is done, let it get cool before you turn it out. Eat it with butter and sugar stirred together to a cream, and flavoured with lemon.

FLOUR HASTY PUDDING.

Tie together half a dozen peach leaves, put them into a quart of milk, and set it on the fire to boil. When it has come to a hard boil, take out the leaves, but let the pot remain boiling on the fire. Then with a large wooden spoon in one hand, and some wheat flour in the other, thicken and stir it till it is about the consistence of a boiled custard. Afterwards throw in, one at a time, a dozen small bits of butter rolled in a thick coat of flour. You may enrich it by stirring in a beaten egg or two, a few minutes before you take it from the fire. When done, pour it into a deep dish, and strew brown sugar thickly over the top. Eat it warm.

INDIAN MUSH.

Have ready on the fire a pot of boiling water. Stir into it by degrees (a handful at a time) sufficient Indian meal to make it very thick, and then add a very small portion of salt. You must keep the pot boiling on the fire all the time you are throwing in the meal; and between every handful, stir very hard with the mush-stick, (a round stick flattened at one end,) that the mush may not be lumpy. After it is sufficiently thick, keep it boiling for an hour longer, stirring it occasionally. Then cover the pot, and hang it higher up the chimney, so as to simmer slowly or keep hot for another hour. The goodness of mush depends greatly on its being long and thoroughly boiled. If sufficiency cooked, it is wholesome and nutritious, but exactly the reverse, if made in haste. It is not too long to have it altogether three of four hours over the fire; on the contrary it will be much the better for it.

Eat it warm; either with milk, or cover your plate with mush, make a hole in the middle, put some butter in the hole and fill it up with molasses.

Cold mush that has been left, may be cut into slices and fried in butter.

Burgoo is made precisely in the same manner as mush, but with oatmeal instead of Indian.

A BAKED INDIAN PUDDING.

Cut up a quarter of a pound of butter in a pint of molasses, and warm them together till the butter is melted. Boil a quart of milk; and while scalding hot, pour it slowly over a pint of sifted Indian meal, and stir in the molasses and butter. Cover it, and let it steep for an hour. Then take off the cover, and set the mixture to cool. When it is cold, beat six eggs, and stir them gradually into it; add a table-spoonful of mixed cinnamon and nutmeg; and the grated peel of a lemon. Stir the whole very hard; put it into a buttered dish, and bake it two hours. Serve it up hot, and eat it with wine sauce, or with butter and molasses.

A BOILED INDIAN PUDDING.

Chop very fine a quarter of a pound of beef suet, and mix it with a pint of sifted Indian meal. Boil a quart of milk with some pieces of cinnamon broken up; strain it, and while it is hot, stir in gradually the meal and suet; add half a pint of molasses. Cover the mixture and set it away for an hour; then put it to cool. Beat six eggs, and stir them gradually into the mixture when it is cold; add a grated nutmeg, and the grated peel of a lemon. Tie the pudding in a cloth that has been dipped in hot water and floured; and leave plenty of room for it to swell. Secure it well at the tying place lest the water should get in, which will infallibly spoil it. Put it into a pot of boiling water, (which must be replenished as it boils away,) and boil it four hours at least; but five or six will be better. To have an Indian pudding *very good*, it should be mixed the night before, (all except the eggs,) and put on to boil early in the morning. Do not take it out of the pot till immediately before it is wanted. Eat it with wine sauce, or with molasses and butter.

INDIAN PUDDING WITHOUT EGGS.

Boil some cinnamon in a quart of milk, and then strain it. While the milk is hot, stir into it a pint of molasses, and then add by degrees a quart or more of Indian meal so as to make a thick batter. It will be much improved by the grated peel and juice of a large lemon or orange. Tie it very securely in a thick cloth, leaving room for it to swell, and pasting up the tying-place with a lump of flour and water. Put it into a pot of boiling water, (having ready a kettle to fill it up as it boils away,) hang it over a good fire, and keep it boiling hard for four or five hours. Eat it warm with molasses and butter.

This is a very economical, and not an unpalatable pudding; and may be found convenient when it is difficult to obtain eggs.

A BAKED PLUM PUDDING.

Grate all the crumb of a stale six cent loaf; boil a quart of rich milk, and pour it boiling hot over the grated bread; cover it, and let it steep for an hour; then set it out to cool. In the mean time prepare half a pound of currants, picked, washed, and dried; half a pound of raisins, stoned and cut in half; and a quarter of a pound of citron cut in large slips; also, two nutmegs beaten to a powder; and a table-spoonful of mace and cinnamon powdered and mixed together. Crush with a rolling-pin half a pound of sugar, and cut up half a pound of butter. When the bread and milk is uncovered to cool, mix with it the butter, sugar, spice and citron; adding a glass of brandy, and a glass of white wine. Beat eight eggs very light, and when the milk is quite cold, stir them gradually into the mixture. Then add, by degrees, the raisins and currants, (which must be previously dredged with flour) and stir the whole very hard. Put it into a buttered dish, and bake it two hours. Send it to table warm, and eat it with wine sauce, or with wine and sugar only.

In making this pudding, you may substitute for the butter, half a pound of beef suet minced as fine as possible. It will be found best to prepare the ingredients the day before, covering them closely and putting them away.

A BOILED PLUM PUDDING.

Grate the crumb of a twelve cent loaf of bread, and boil a quart of rich milk with a small bunch of peach leaves in it, then strain it and set it out to cool. Pick, wash and dry a pound of currants, and stone and cut in half a pound of raisins; strew over them three large table-spoonfuls of flour. Roll fine a pound of brown sugar, and mince as fine as possible three quarters of a pound of beef suet. Prepare two beaten nutmegs, and a large table-spoonful of powdered mace and cinnamon; also the grated peel and the juice of two large lemons or oranges. Beat ten eggs very light, and (when it is cold) stir them gradually into the milk, alternately with the suet and grated bread.

Add, by degrees, the sugar, fruit, and spice, with a large glass of brandy, and one of white wine. Mix the whole very well, and stir it hard. Then put it into a thick cloth that has been scalded and floured; leave room for it to swell, and tie it very firmly, pasting the tying-place with a small lump of moistened flour. Put the pudding into a large pot of boiling water, and boil it steadily five hours, replenishing the pot occasionally from a boiling kettle. Turn the pudding frequently in the pot. Prepare half a pound of citron cut in slips, and half a pound of almonds blanched and split in half lengthways. Stick the almonds and the citron all over the outside of the pudding as soon as you take it out of the cloth. Send it to table hot, and eat it with wine sauce, or with cold wine and sugar.

If there is enough of the pudding left, it may be cut in slices, and fried in butter next day.

All the ingredients of this plum pudding (except the eggs) should be prepared the day before, otherwise it cannot be made in time to allow of its being sufficiently boiled.

We have known of a very rich plum pudding being mixed in England and sent to America in a covered bowl; it arrived perfectly good after a month's voyage, the season being winter.

A BAKED APPLE PUDDING.

Take nine large pippin apples; pare and core them whole. Set them in the bottom of a large deep dish, and pour round them a very little water, just enough to keep them from burning. Put them into an oven, and let them bake about half an hour. In the mean time, mix three table-spoonfuls of flour with a quart of milk, a quarter of a pound of brown sugar, and a tea-spoonful of mixed spice. Beat seven eggs very light, and stir them gradually into the milk. Then take out the dish of apples, (which by this time should be half baked,) and fill up the holes from whence you extracted the cores, with brown sugar; pressing down into each a slice of fresh lemon. Pour the batter round the apples; put the dish again into the oven, and let it bake another half hour; but not long enough for the apples to fall to pieces; as they should, when done, be soft throughout, but quite whole. Send it to table warm.

This is sometimes called a *Bird's Nest Pudding.*

It will be much improved by previously boiling in the milk a small handful of peach leaves. Let it get cold before you stir in the eggs.

BOILED APPLE PUDDING.

Pare, core, and quarter as many fine juicy apples as will weigh two pounds when done. Strew among them a quarter of a pound of brown sugar, and add a grated nutmeg, and the juice and yellow peel of a large lemon. Prepare a paste of suet and flour, in the proportion of a pound of chopped suet to two pounds of flour. Roll it out of moderate thickness; lay the apples in the centre, and close the paste nicely over them in the form of a large dumpling; tie it in a cloth and boil it three hours. Send it to table hot, and eat with it cream sauce, or with butter and sugar.

Any fruit pudding may be made in a similar manner.

AN EASTERN PUDDING.

Make a paste of a pound of flour and half a pound of minced suet; and roll it out thin into a square or oblong sheet; trim off the edges so as to make it an even shape. Spread thickly over it some marmalade, or cold stewed fruit, (which must be made very sweet,) either apple, peach, plum, gooseberry or cranberry. Roll up the paste, with the fruit spread on it, into a scroll. Secure each end by putting on nicely a thin round piece rolled out from the trimmings that you cut off the edges of the sheet. Put the pudding into a cloth, and boil it at least three hours. Serve it up hot, and eat it with cream sauce, or with butter and sugar.

APPLE DUMPLINGS.

Take large fine juicy apples. Pare them, and extract the cores without dividing the apple. Fill each hole with brown sugar, and some chips of lemon peel. Also squeeze in some lemon juice. Or you may fill the cavities with raspberry jam, or with any sort of marmalade. Have ready a paste, made in the proportion of a pound of suet, chopped as fine as possible, to two pounds and a half of sifted flour, well mixed, and wetted with as little water as possible. Roll out the paste to a moderate thickness, and cut it into circular pieces, allowing two pieces to each dumpling. Lay your apple on one piece, and put another piece on the top, closing the paste round the sides with your fingers, so as to cover the apple entirely. This is a better way than gathering up the paste at one end, as the dumpling is less liable to burst. Boil each dumpling in a small coarse cloth, which has first been dipped in hot water. There should always be a set of cloths kept for the purpose. Tie them tightly, leaving a small space for the dumpling to swell. Plaster a little flour on the inside of each tying place to prevent the water from getting in. Have ready a pot of boiling water. Put in the dumplings and boil them from three quarters to an hour. Send them to table hot in a covered dish. Do not take them up till a moment before they are wanted.

Eat them with cream and sugar, or with butter and sugar.

You may make the paste with butter instead of suet, allowing a pound of butter to two pounds and a quarter of flour. But when paste is to be boiled, suet will make it much lighter and finer than butter.

Apple dumplings may be made in a very plain manner with potato paste, and boiled without cloths, dredging the outside of each dumpling with flour. They should boil about three quarters of an hour when without cloths.

The apples for dumplings should always be whole, (except the cores:) for if quartered, the pieces will separate in boiling and break through the crust. The apples should never be sweet ones.

RICE DUMPLINGS.

Pick and wash a pound of rice, and boil it gently in two quarts of water till it becomes dry; keeping the pot well covered, and not stirring it. Then take it off the fire, and spread it out to cool on the bottom, of an inverted sieve; loosening the grains lightly with a fork, that all the moisture may evaporate. Pare a dozen pippins or other, large juicy apples, and scoop out the core. Then fill up the cavity with marmalade, or with lemon and sugar. Cover every apple all over with a thick coating of the boiled rice. Tie up each in a separate, cloth, [Footnote: Your pudding and dumpling cloths should be squares of coarse thick linen, hemmed, and with tape strings sewed to them. After using, they should be washed, dried, and ironed; and kept in one of the kitchen drawers, that they may be always ready when wanted.] and put them into a pot of cold water. They will require about an hour and a quarter after they begin to boil; perhaps longer.

Turn them out on a large dish, and be careful in doing so not to break the dumplings. Eat them with cream sauce, or with wine sauce, or with butter, sugar, and nutmeg beaten together.

PIGEON DUMPLINGS OR PUDDINGS.

Take four pigeons and stuff them with chopped oysters, seasoned with pepper, salt, mace, and nutmeg. Score the breasts, and loosen all the joints with a sharp knife, as if you were going to carve them for eating; but do not cut them quite apart. Make a sufficient quantity of nice suet paste, allowing a pound of suet to two pounds of flour; roll it out thick, and divide it into four. Lay one pigeon on each sheet of the paste with the back downwards, and put at the lower part of the breast a piece of butter rolled in flour. Close the paste over the pigeon in the form of a dumpling or small pudding; pouring in at the last a very little cold water to add to the gravy. Tie each dumpling in a cloth, put them into a pot of hot water, and boil them two hours. Send them to table with made gravy in a boat.

Partridges or quails may be cooked in this manner; also chickens, which must be accompanied by egg sauce. These dumplings or puddings will be found very good.

FINE SUET DUMPLINGS.

Grate the crumb of a stale six cent loaf, and mix it with nearly as much beef suet, chopped as fine as possible. Add a grated nutmeg, and two large table-spoonfuls of sugar. Beat four eggs with four table-spoonfuls of white wine or brandy. Mix all well together to a stiff paste. Flour your hands, and make up the mixture into balls or dumplings about the size of turkey eggs. Have ready a pot of boiling water. Put the dumplings into cloths, and let them boil about half an hour. Serve them hot, and eat them with wine sauce.

PLAIN SUET DUMPLINGS.

Sift two pounds of flour into a pan, and add a salt-spoon of salt. Mince very fine one pound of beef suet, and rub it into the flour. Make it into a stiff dough with a little cold water. Then roll it out an inch thick or rather more. Cut it into dumplings with the edge of a tumbler. Put them into a pot of boiling water, and let them boil an hour and a half. Send them to table hot, to eat with boiled loin of mutton, or with molasses after the meat is removed.

INDIAN DUMPLINGS.

Take a pint of milk, and four eggs well beaten. Stir them together, and add a salt-spoon of salt. Then mix in as much sifted Indian meal as will make a stiff dough. Flour your hands; divide the dough into equal portions, and make it into balls about the size of a goose egg. Flatten each with the rolling-pin, tie them in cloths, and put them into a pot of boiling water.

They will boil in a short time. Take care not to let them go to pieces by keeping them too long in the pot.

Serve them up hot, and eat them with corned pork, or with bacon. Or you may eat them with molasses and butter after the meat is removed.

If to be eaten without meat, you may mix in the dough a quarter of a pound of finely chopped suet.

LIVER DUMPLINGS.

Take a calf's liver, and chop it very fine. Mix with it half a pound of beef suet chopped line also; half a pound of flour; two minced onions; a handful of bread-crumbs; a table-spoonful of chopped parsley and sweet marjoram mixed; a few blades of mace and a few cloves powdered; and a little pepper and salt. Mix all well together. Wet the mixture with six eggs well beaten, and make it up into dumplings, with your hands well floured. Have ready a large pot of boiling water. Drop the dumplings into it with a ladle, and let them boil an hour. Have ready bread-crumbs browned in butter to poor over them before they go to table.

HAM DUMPLINGS.

Chop some cold ham, the fat and lean in equal proportions. Season it with pepper and minced sage. Make a crust, allowing half a pound of chopped suet; or half a pound of butter to a pound of flour. Roll it out thick, and divide it into equal portions. Put some minced ham into each, and close up the crust. Have ready a pot of boiling water, and put in the dumplings. Boil them about three quarters of an hour.

LIGHT DUMPLINGS.

Mix together as much grated bread, butter and beaten egg (seasoned with powdered cinnamon) as will make a stiff paste. Stir it well. Make the mixture into round dumplings, with your hands well floured. Tie up each in a separate cloth, and boil them a short time,—about fifteen minutes. Eat them with wine sauce, or with molasses and butter.

PLAIN FRITTERS.

Beat seven eggs very light, and stir them gradually into a quart of milk; add, by degrees, three quarters of a pound, or a pint and a half of sifted flour. Beat the whole very hard. Have ready in a frying-pan over the fire, a large quantity of lard. When the lard has come to a hard boil, begin to put in the fritters; allowing for each about a jill of batter, or half a large tea-cup full. They do not require turning, and will be done in a few minutes. Fry as many at a time as the pan will hold. Send them to table hot, and eat them with powdered cinnamon, sugar, and white wine. Let fresh hot ones be sent in as they are wanted; they chill and become heavy immediately.

Begin to fry the fritters as soon as the batter is mixed, as it will fall by setting. Near a pound and a half of lard will be required for the above quantity of fritters.

APPLE FRITTERS.

Pave, core, and parboil (in a very little water) some large juicy pippins. When half done, take them out, drain them, and mince them very fine. Make a batter according to the preceding receipt; adding some lemon juice and grated lemon-peel. Stir into the batter a sufficient quantity of the minced apple to make it very thick. Then fry the fritters in hot lard as before directed. Eat them with nutmeg and sugar.

PLAIN PANCAKES.

Sift half a pound or a pint of flour. Beat seven eggs very light, and stir them gradually into a quart of rich milk. Then add by degrees the flour, so as to make a thin batter. Mix it very smooth, pressing out all the lumps with the back of a spoon. Set the frying-pan over the fire, and when it is hot, grease it with a spoonful of lard. Then put in a ladle full of the batter, and fry it of a light brown, turning it with care to prevent its breaking. Make each pancake large enough to cover the bottom of a dessert plate; greasing the pan every time. Send them to table hot, accompanied by powdered sugar and nutmeg mixed in a small glass bowl. Have wine with them also.

SWEETMEAT PANCAKES.

Take a large red beet-root that has been boiled tender; cut it up and pound it in a mortar till you have sufficient juice for colouring the pancakes. Then make a batter as in the preceding receipt, and stir into it at the last enough of the beet juice to give it a fine pink colour. Or instead of the beet juice, you may use a little cochineal dissolved in a very small quantity of brandy. Fry the pancakes in a pan greased with lard or fresh butter; and as fast as they are done, spread thickly over them raspberry jam or any sort of marmalade. Then roll them up nicely, and trim off the ends. Lay them, side by side, on a large dish, and strew powdered sugar over them. Send them to table hot, and eat them with sweetened cream.

PLAIN CUSTARDS.

Tie together six or eight peach leaves, and boil them in a quart of milk with a large stick of cinnamon broken up. If you cannot procure peach leaves, substitute a handful of peach-kernels or bitter almonds, or a vanilla bean split in pieces. When it has boiled hard, strain the milk and set it away to cool. Beat very light eight eggs, and stir them by degrees into the milk when it is quite cold, (if warm, the eggs will curdle it, and cause whey at the bottom,) and add gradually a quarter of a pound of sugar. Fill your cups with it; set them in a Dutch-oven, and pour round them boiling water sufficient to reach nearly to the tops of the cups. Put hot coals under the oven and on the lid, (which must be previously heated by standing it up before a hot fire,) and bake the custards about twenty minutes. Send them to table cold, with nutmeg grated over each. Or you may bake the whole in one large dish.

SOFT CUSTARDS.

Are made in the above manner, except that to a quart of milk you must have twelve yolks of eggs, and no whites. You may devote to this purpose the yolks that are left when you have used the whites for cocoa-nut or almond puddings, or for lady cake or maccaroons.

BOILED CUSTARDS.

Beat eight eggs very light, omitting the whites of four. Mix them gradually with a quart of cold milk and a quarter of a pound of sugar. Put the mixture into a sauce-pan with a bunch of peach leaves, or a handful of broken up peach-kernels or bitter almonds; the yellow peel of a. lemon, and a handful of broken cinnamon; or you may boil in it a vanilla bean. Set it on hot coals, and simmer it slowly, stirring it all the time. As soon as it comes to a boil, take it immediately off the fire, or it will curdle and be lumpy. Then strain it; add eight or ten drops of oil of lemon, and put it into glass cups. You may lay in the bottom of each cup a maccaroon soaked in wine. Grate nutmeg over the top, and send it to table cold. Eat it with tarts or sweetmeats.

RICE CUSTARD.

Boil some rice in milk till it is quite dry; then put it into small tea-cups, (pressing it down hard,) and when it is cold and has taken the shape of the cups, turn it out into a deep dish, and pour a boiled custard round it. Lay on the top of each lump of rice a piece of preserved quince or peach, or a piece of fruit jelly. In boiling the rice, you may mix with, it raisins or currants; if so, omit the sweetmeats on the top.

Another way of boiling custard is to put the mixture into a pitches, set it in a vessel of boiling water, place it on hot coals or in a stove, and let it boil slowly, stirring it all the time.

SNOWBALL CUSTARD.

Make a boiled custard as in the preceding receipts; and when it is done and quite cold, put it into a deep glass dish. Beat to a stiff froth the four whites of eggs that have been omitted in the custard, adding eight or ten drops of oil of lemon. Drop the froth in balls on the top of the dish of custard, heaping and forming them with a spoon into a regular size and shape. Do not let them touch each other. You may lay a fresh, rose leaf on the top of every one.

APPLE CUSTARD.

Pare, core, and quarter a dozen large juicy pippins. Strew among them the yellow peel of a large lemon pared very thin; and stew them till tender, in a very small portion of water. When done, mash them smooth with the back of a spoon; (you must have a pint and a half of the stewed apple;) mix a quarter of a pound of sugar with them, and set them away till cold. Beat six eggs very light, and stir them gradually into a quart of rich milk, alternately with the stewed apple. Put the mixture into cups, or into a deep dish, and bake it about twenty minutes. Send it to table cold, with nutmeg grated over the top.

LEMON CUSTARD.

Take four large ripe lemons, and roll them under your hand on the table to increase the juice. Then squeeze them into a bowl, and mix with the juice a very small tea-cup full of cold water. Use none of the peel. Add gradually sufficient sugar to make it very sweet. Beat twelve eggs till quite light, and then stir the lemon juice gradually into them, beating very hard at the last. Put the mixture into cups, and bake it ten minutes. When done, grate nutmeg over the top of each, and set them among ice, or in a very cold place.

These custards being made without milk, can be prepared at a short notice; they will be found very fine.

Orange custards may be made in the same manner.

GOOSEBERRY CUSTARD.

Top and tail two quarts of green gooseberries. Stew them in a very little water; stirring and mashing them frequently. When they have stewed till entirely to pieces, take them out, and with a wooden spoon press the pulp through a cullender. Stir in (while the pulp is hot) a table-spoonful of butter, and sufficient sugar to make it very sweet. Beat six eggs very light. Simmer the gooseberry pulp over a gentle fire, and gradually stir the beaten eggs into it. When it comes to a boil, take it off immediately, stir it very hard, and set it out to cool. Serve it up cold in glasses or custard cups, grating some nutmeg over each.

ALMOND CUSTARD.

Scald and blanch half a pound of shelled sweet almonds, and three ounces of shelled bitter almonds; throwing them as you do them into a large bowl of cold water. Then pound them one at a time in a mortar; pouring in frequently a little rose water to prevent their oiling, and becoming dark-coloured and heavy. Melt a quarter of a pound of loaf-sugar in a quart of cream or rich milk, and stir in by degrees the pounded almonds. Beat ten eggs very light, and stir them gradually into the mixture; adding a powdered nutmeg, and a tea-spoonful of powdered mace and cinnamon mixed. Then put the whole into a pitcher, and place it in a kettle or pan of boiling water, the water coming up to the lower part of the neck of the pitcher. Set it over hot coals, and let it boil (stirring it all the time) till it is quite thick, but not till it curdles. Then take the pitcher out of the water; pour the custard into a large bowl, and stir it till it cools. Put it into glass cups, and send it to table cold. Sweeten some cream or white of egg. Beat it to stiff froth, and pile it on the top of the custards.

BOILED COCOA-NUT CUSTARD.

To a pound of grated cocoa-nut allow a pint of unskimmed milk, and six ounces of white sugar. Beat very light the yolks of six eggs. Stir them gradually into the milk, alternately with the cocoa-nut and sugar. Put the mixture into a pitcher; set it in a vessel of boiling water; place it on hot coals, and simmer it till it is very smooth and thick; stirring it all the time. As soon as it comes to a hard boil, take it off the fire; pour it into a large bowl, and set it out to cool. When cold, put it into glass cups. Beat to a stiff froth the white of egg that was left, and pile it on the custards.

BAKED COCOA-NUT CUSTARD.

Grate as much cocoa-nut as will weigh a pound. Mix half a pound of powdered white sugar with the milk of the cocoa-nut, or with a pint of cream; adding two table-spoonfuls of rose water. Then stir in gradually a pint of rich milk. Beat to a stiff froth the whites of eight eggs, and stir them into the milk and sugar, a little at a time, alternately with the grated cocoa-nut; add a tea-spoonful of powdered nutmeg and cinnamon. Then put the mixture into cups, and bake them twenty minutes in a Dutch oven half filled with boiling water. When cold, grate loaf-sugar over them.

CHOCOLATE CUSTARD.

Scrape fine a quarter of a pound of the best chocolate, and pour on it a tea-cup of boiling water. Cover it, and let it stand by the fire till it has dissolved, stirring it twice. Beat eight eggs very light, omitting the whites of two. Stir them by degrees into a quart of cream or rich milk, alternately with the melted chocolate, and three table-spoonfuls of powdered white sugar. Pat the mixture into cups, and bake it about ten minutes. Send them to table cold, with sweetened cream, or white of egg beaten to a stiff froth, and heaped on the top of each custard.

MACCAROON CUSTARDS.

These must he made in china custard cups. Put a maccaroon in the bottom of each cup, and pour on it a table-spoonful of white wine. Mix together a pint of cream, and a pint of milk; and boil them with a large stick of cinnamon broken up, and a small bunch of peach leaves or a handful of broken bitter almonds. Then strain the milk; stir in a quarter of a pound of white sugar, and set it away to cool. Beat very light eight eggs, (omitting the whites of four,) and stir them gradually into the cream and milk when quite cold. Fill your cups with the mixture, (leaving the maccaroons at the bottom,) and set them in a Dutch oven or iron baking pan, which must be half full of boiling water. Heat the oven-lid first, by standing it up before a hot fire; then put it on, spreading coals over the top. Place sufficient coals under the oven, and bake the custards about ten minutes. When cold, heap beaten white of egg on the top of each. These custards are very fine.

SYLLABUB, OR WHIPT CREAM.

Pare off very thin the yellow rind of four large lemons, And lay it in the bottom of a deep dish. Squeeze the juice of the lemons into a large bowl containing a pint of white wine, and sweeten it with half a pound of powdered loaf-sugar Then, by degrees, mix in a quart of cream. Pour the whole into the dish in which you have laid the lemon-peel, and let the mixture stand untouched for three hours. Then beat it with rods to a stiff froth, (first taking out the lemon-peel,) and having put into each of your glasses a table-spoonful or more of fruit jelly, heap the syllabub upon it so as to stand up high at the top. This syllabub, if it can be kept in a cold place, may be made the day before you want to use it.

COUNTRY SYLLABUB.

Mix half a pound of white sugar with a pint of fine sweet cider, or of white wine; and grate in a nutmeg. Prepare them in a large bowl, just before milking time. Then let it be taken to the cow, and have about three pints milked into it; stirring it occasionally with a spoon. Let it be eaten before the froth subsides. If you use cider, a little brandy will improve it.

A TRIFLE.

Place half a pound of maccaroons or Naples biscuits at the bottom of a large glass bowl. Pour on them as much white wine as will cover and dissolve them. Make a rich custard, flavoured with bitter almonds or peach leaves; and pour it when cold on the maccaroons; the custard may be either baked or boiled. Then add a layer of marmalade or jam. Take a quart of cream, mix with it a quarter of a pound of sugar, and half a pint of white wine, and whip it with rods to a stiff froth; laying the froth (as you proceed) on an inverted sieve, with a dish under it to catch the cream that drips through; which must be saved and whipped over again. Instead of rods you may use a little tin churn. Pile the frothed cream upon the marmalade in a high pyramid. To ornament it,—take preserved water-melon rind that has been cut into leaves or flowers; split them nicely to make them thinner and lighter; place a circle or wreath of them round the heap of frothed cream, interspersing them with spots of stiff red currant jelly. Stick on the top of the pyramid a sprig of real flowers.

FLOATING ISLAND.

Take a quart of rich cream, and divide it in half. Sweeten one pint of it with loaf-sugar, and stir into it sufficient currant jelly to colour it of a fine pink. Put it into a glass bowl, and place in the centre a pile of sliced almond-sponge cake, or of lady cake; every slice spread thickly with raspberry jam or marmalade, and laid evenly one on another. Have ready the other pint of cream, flavoured with a few drops of oil of lemon, and beaten with rods to a stiff froth. Heap it all over the pile of cake, so as entirely to cover it.

A RASPBERRY CHARLOTTE.

Take a dozen of the square or oblong sponge-cakes that are commonly called Naples biscuits. They should be quite fresh. Spread over each a thick layer of raspberry jam, and place them in the bottom and round the sides of a glass bowl. Take the whites of six eggs, and mix with them six table-spoonfuls of raspberry or currant jelly. Beat the egg and jelly with rods till very light, and then fill up the bowl with it. For this purpose, cream (if you can conveniently procure it) is still better than white of egg.

You may make a charlotte with any sort of jam, marmalade, or fruit jelly. It can be prepared at a short notice, and is very generally liked.

A PLUM CHARLOTTE.

Stone a quart of ripe plums, and stew them with a pound of brown sugar. Cut slices of bread and butter and lay them in the bottom and round the sides of a large bowl or deep dish. Pour in the plums boiling hot, cover the bowl, and set it away to cool gradually. When, quite cold, send it to table, and eat it with cream.

CLOTTED CREAM.

Mix together a jill of rich milk, a large wine glass of rose water, and four ounces of white sugar. Add to it the beaten yolks of two eggs. Stir the mixture into a quart of the best cream; set it over hot coals, and let it just come to a boil, stirring it all the time. Then take it off, pour it into a glass bowl, and set it away to get cold. Eat it with fresh strawberries, raspberries, or with any sort of sweetmeats.

LEMON CREAM.

Beat well together a quart of thick cream and the yolks of eight eggs. Then gradually beat in half a pound of powdered loaf-sugar, and the grated rind of three large lemons. Put the mixture into a porcelain skillet, and set it on hot coals till it comes to a boil; then take it off, and stir it till nearly cold. Squeeze the juice of the lemons into a bowl; pour the cream upon it, and continue to stir it till quite cold. You may serve it up in a glass bowl, in glass cups, or in jelly glasses. Eat it with tarts or sweetmeats.

ORANGE CREAM.

Beat very light six eggs, omitting the whites of two. Have ready a pint of orange juice, and stir it gradually into the beaten egg, alternately with a pound of powdered loaf-sugar. Put into a porcelain skillet the yellow rind of one orange, pared very thin; pour the mixture upon it, and set it over a slow fire. Simmer it steadily, stirring it all the time; but when nearly ready to boil, take it off, remove the orange-peel, and put the mixture into glasses to get cold.

CURDS AND WHEY.

Take a piece of rennet about three inches square, and wash it in two or three cold waters to get off the salt; wipe it dry, and fasten a string to one corner of it. Have ready in a deep dish or pan, a quart of unskimmed milk that has been warmed but not boiled. Put the rennet into it, leaving the string hanging out over the side, that you may know where to find it. Cover the pan, and set it by the fire-side or in some other warm place. When the milk becomes a firm mass of curd, and the whey looks clear and greenish, remove the rennet as gently as possible, pulling it out by the string; and set the pan in ice, or in a very cold place. Send to table with it a small pitcher of white wine, sugar and nutmeg mixed together; or a bowl of sweetened cream, with nutmeg grated over it.

You may keep rennet in white wine; cutting it in small pieces, and putting it into a glass jar with wine enough to cover it well. Either the wine or the rennet will be found good for turning milk; but do not put in both together, or the curd will become so hard and tough, as to be uneatable.

Rennets properly prepared and dried, are sold constantly in the Philadelphia markets. The cost is trifling; and it is well to have one always in the house, in case of being wanted to make whey for sick persons. They will keep a year or more.

LEMON ICE CREAM.

Have ready two quarts of very rich thick cream, and take out a pint. Stir gradually into the pint, a pound of the best loaf-sugar powdered fine; and the grated rind and the juice of four ripe lemons of the largest size, or of five or six smaller ones. If you cannot procure the fruit, you may flavour the cream with essence or oil of lemon; a tea-spoonful or more, according to its strength. The strongest and best essence of lemon is the white or whitish; when tinged with green, it is comparatively weak, having been diluted with water; if quite green, a large tea-spoonful will not communicate as much flavour as five or six drops of the white. After you have mixed the pint of cream with the sugar and lemon, beat it gradually and hard into the remaining cream, that is, the three pints. Cover it, and let it stand to infuse from half an hour to an hour. Then taste it, and if you think it necessary, stir in a little more lemon juice or a little more sugar. Strain it into the freezer through a fine strainer, (a tin one with small close holes is best,) to get rid of the grated lemon-peel, which if left in would prevent the cream from being smooth. Cover the freezer, and stand it in the ice cream tub, which should be filled with a mixture, in equal quantities, of coarse salt, and ice broken up as small as possible, that it may lie close and compact round the freezer, and thus add to its coldness. Snow, when it can be procured, is still better than ice to mix with the salt. It should be packed closely into the tub, and pressed down hard. Keep turning the freezer about by the handle till the cream is frozen, which it will generally be in two hours. Occasionally open the lid and scrape down the cream from the sides with a long-handled tin spoon. Take care that no salt gets in, or the cream will be spoiled. When it is entirely frozen, take it out of the freezer and put it into your mould; set it again in the tub, (which must be filled with fresh ice and salt,) and leave it undisturbed till you want it for immediate use. This second freezing, however, should not continue longer than two hours, or the cream will become inconveniently and unpleasantly hard, and have much of the flavour frozen out of it. Place the mould in the ice tub, with the head downwards, and cover the tub with pieces of old carpet while the second freezing is going on. When it has arrived at the proper consistence, and it is time to serve it up, dip a cloth in hot water, and wrap it round the mould for a few moments, to loosen the cream and make it come out easily; setting the mould on a glass or china dish. If a pyramid or obelisk mould, lift it carefully off the top. If the mould or form represents doves, dolphins, lap-dogs, fruit baskets, &c. it will open down the middle, and must be taken off in that manner. Serve it up immediately lest it begin to melt. Send round sponge-cake with it, and wine or cordials immediately after.

If you have no moulds, but intend serving it up in a large bowl or in glasses, it must still be frozen twice over; otherwise it can have no smoothness, delicacy, or consistence, but will be rough and coarse, and feel in the mouth like broken icicles. The second freezing (if you have no mould) must be done in the freezer, which should be washed out, and set again in the tub with fresh ice and salt. Cover it closely, and let the cream stand in it untouched, but not less than two hours. When you put it into glasses, heap it high on the top.

Begin to make ice cream about five or six hours before it is wanted for use. If you commence it too early, it may probably be injured by having to remain too long in the second freezing, as it must not be turned out till a few moments before it is served up. In damp weather it requires a longer time to freeze.

If cream is scarce, mix with it an equal quantity of rich milk, and then add, for each quart, two table-spoonfuls of powdered arrow-root rubbed smooth in a little cold milk. Orange ice cream is made in the same manner as lemon.

STRAWBERRY ICE CREAM.

Take two quarts of ripe strawberries; hull them, and put them into a deep dish, strewing among them half a pound of powdered loaf-sugar. Cover them, and let them stand an hour or two. Then mash them through a sieve till you have pressed out all the juice, and stir into it half a pound more of powdered sugar, or enough to make it very sweet, and like a thick syrup. Then mix it by degrees with two quarts of rich cream, beating it in very hard. Put it into a freezer, and proceed as in the foregoing receipt. In two hours, remove it to a mould, or take it out and return it again to the freezer with fresh salt and ice, that it may be frozen a second time. In two hours more, it should be ready to turn out.

RASPBERRY ICE CREAM.

Is made according to the preceding receipt.

PINE-APPLE ICE CREAM.

To each quart of cream allow a large ripe pine-apple, and a pound of powdered loaf-sugar. Pare the pine-apple, slice it very thin, and mince it small. Lay it in a deep dish and strew the sugar among it. Cover the dish, and let the pine-apple lie in the sugar for two or three hours. Then strain it through a sieve, mashing and pressing out all the juice. Stir the juice gradually into the cream, beating it hard. Put it into the freezer, and let it be twice frozen before it is served up.

VANILLA ICE CREAM.

Split up half a vanilla bean, and boil it slowly in half a pint of milk till all the flavour is drawn out, which you may know by tasting it. Then mix into the milk half a pound of powdered loaf-sugar, and stir it very hard into a quart of rich cream. Put it into the freezer, and proceed as directed in the receipt for Lemon Ice Cream; freezing it twice.

ALMOND ICE CREAM.

Take six ounces of bitter almonds, (sweet ones will not do,) blanch them, and pound them in a mortar, adding by degrees a little rose water. Then boil them gently in a pint of cream till you find that it is highly flavoured with them. Then pour the cream into a bowl, stir in a pound of powdered loaf-sugar, cover it, and set it away to cool gradually; when it is cold, strain it and then stir it gradually and hard into three pints of cream. Put it into the freezer, and proceed as directed in the first ice cream receipt. Freeze it twice. It will be found very fine.

Send round always with ice cream, sponge cake or Savoy biscuits. Afterwards wine, and cordials, or liqueurs as they are now generally called.

ICE ORANGEADE.

Take a pint and a half of orange juice, and mix it with half a pint of clear or filtered water. Stir in half a pound of powdered loaf-sugar. Pare very thin the yellow rind of six deep-coloured oranges, cut in pieces, and lay it at the bottom of a bowl or tureen. Pour the orange juice and sugar upon it; cover it, and let it infuse an hour. Then strain the liquid into a freezer, and proceed as for ice cream. When it is frozen, put it into a mould, (it will look best in the form of a pine-apple,) and freeze it a second time. Serve it in glass cups, with any sort of very nice sweet cakes.

ICE LEMONADE.

May be made in the above manner, but with a larger proportion of sugar.

The juice of pine-apples, strawberries, raspberries, currants and cherries, may be prepared and frozen according to the above receipts. They will freeze in a shorter time than if mixed with cream, but are very inferior in richness.

BLANC-MANGE.

Put into a bowl an ounce of isinglass; (in warm weather you must take an ounce and a quarter;) pour on as much rose water as will cover the isinglass, and set it on hot ashes to dissolve. [Footnote: You may make the stock for blanc-mange without isinglass, by boiling four calves' feet in two quarts of water till reduced one half, and till the meat is entirely to rags. Strain it, and set it away till next day. Then clear it from the fat and sediment; cut it into pieces and boil it with the cream and the other ingredients. When you take it from the fire, and strain it into the pitcher, keep stirring it till it gets cold.] Blanch a quarter of a pound of shelled almonds, (half sweet and half bitter,) and beat them to a paste in a mortar, (one at a time,) moistening them all the while with a little rose water. Stir the almonds by degrees into a quart of cream, alternately with half a pound of powdered white sugar; add a large tea-spoonful of beaten mace. Put in the melted isinglass, and stir the whole very hard. Then put it into a porcelain skillet, and let it boil fast for a quarter of an hour. Then strain it into a pitcher, and pour it into your moulds, which must first be wetted with cold water. Let it stand in a cool place undisturbed, till it has entirely congealed, which will be in about five hours. Then wrap a cloth dipped in hot water round the moulds, loosen the blanc-mange round the edges with a knife, and turn it out into glass dishes. It is best to make it the day before it is wanted.

Instead of using a figure-mould, you may set it to congeal in tea-cups or wine glasses.

Blanc-mange may be coloured green by mixing with the cream a little juice of spinage; cochineal which has been infused in a little brandy for half an hour, will colour it red; and saffron will give it a bright yellow tinge.

CARRAGEEN BLANC-MANGE.

This is made of a sea-weed resembling moss, that is found in large quantities on some parts of our coast, and is to be purchased in the cities at most of the druggists. Carrageen costs but little, and is considered extremely salutary for persons of delicate constitutions. Its glutinous nature when boiled, renders it very suitable for blanc-mange.

From a quart of rich unskimmed milk take half a pint. Add to the half pint two ounces of bitter almonds, blanched and pounded; half a nutmeg; and a large stick of cinnamon, broken up; also eight or nine blades of mace. Set it in a closed pan over hot coals, and boil it half an hour. In the mean time, wash through two or three *cold* waters half a handful of carrageen, (if you put in too much it will communicate an unpleasant taste to the blanc-mange,) and add it to the pint and a half of cold milk. Then when it is sufficiently flavoured, stir in the boiled milk, adding gradually half a pound of powdered sugar, and mix the whole very well. Set it over the fire, and keep it boiling hard five minutes from the time it has come to a boil. Then strain it into a pitcher; wet your moulds or cups with cold water, put the blanc-mange into them, and leave it undisturbed till it congeals.

After washing the sea-weed, you must drain it well, and shake the water from the sprigs. You may flavour the mixture (*after* it is boiled and strained) with rose-water or peach-water, stirred in at the last.

ARROW ROOT BLANC-MANGE.

Take a tea-cup full of arrow root, put it into a large bowl, and dissolve it in a little cold water. When it is melted, pour off the water, and let the arrow root remain undisturbed. Boil in half a pint of unskimmed milk, (made very sweet with white sugar,) a beaten nutmeg, and eight or nine blades of mace, mixed with the juice and grated peel of a lemon. When it has boiled long enough to be highly flavoured, strain it into a pint and a half of very rich milk or cream, and add a quarter of a pound of sugar. Boil the whole for ten minutes; then strain it, boiling hot, over the arrow roof. Stir it well and frequently till cold; then put it into moulds and let it set to congeal.

JAUNE-MANGE.

Put two ounces of isinglass into a pint of water, and boil it till it has dissolved. Then strain it into a porcelain skillet, and add to it half a pint of white wine; the grated peel and juice of two large deep-coloured oranges; half a pound of loaf-sugar; and the yolks only of eight eggs that have been well beaten. Mix the whole thoroughly; place it on hot coals and simmer it, stirring it all the time till it boils hard. Then take it off directly, strain it, and put it into moulds to congeal.

CALVES' FOOT JELLY.

The best calves' feet for jelly are those that have had the hair removed by scalding, but are not skinned; the skin containing a great deal of glutinous matter. In Philadelphia, unskinned calves' feet are generally to be met with in the lower or Jersey market.

Boil a set of feet in four quarts of cold water; (if the feet have been skinned allow but three quarts;) they should boil slowly till the liquid is reduced to two quarts or one half the original quantity, and the meat has dropped in rags from the bone. Then strain the liquid; measure and set it away in a large earthen pan to get cold; and let it rest till next morning. Then, if you do not find it a firm cake of jelly, boil it over again with an ounce of isinglass, and again set it away till cold and congealed. Remove the sediment from the bottom of the cake of jelly, and carefully scrape off all the fat. The smallest bit of fat will eventually render it dull and cloudy. Press some clean blotting paper all over it to absorb what little grease may yet remain. Then cut the cake of jelly into pieces, and put it into a porcelain kettle to melt over the fire. To each quart allow a pound of broken up loaf-sugar, a pint of Madeira wine, and a large glass of brandy; three large sticks of the best Ceylon cinnamon broken up, (if common cinnamon, use four sticks,) the grated peel and juice of four large lemons; and lastly, the whites of four eggs strained, but not beaten. In breaking the eggs, take care to separate them so nicely that none of the yellow gets into the white; as the smallest portion of yolk of egg will prevent the jelly from being perfectly clear. Mix all the ingredients well together, and put them to the jelly in the kettle. Set it on the fire, and boil it hard for twenty minutes, but do not stir it. Then throw in a tea-cup of cold water, and boil it five minutes longer; then take the kettle off the fire, and set it aside, keeping it closely covered for half an hour; this will improve its clearness. Take a large white flannel jelly-bag; suspend it by the strings to a wooden frame made for such purposes, or to the legs of a table. Pour in the mixture boiling hot, and when it is all in, close up the mouth of the bag that none of the flavour may evaporate. Hang it over a deep white dish or bowl, and let it drip slowly; but on no account squeeze the bag, as that will certainly make the jelly dull and cloudy. If it is not clear the first time, empty the bag, wash it, put in the jelly that has dripped into the dish, and pass it through again. Repeat this till it is clear. You may put it into moulds to congeal, setting them in a cold place. When it is quite firm, wrap a cloth that has been dipped in hot water, round the moulds to make the jelly turn out easily. But it will look much better, and the taste will be more lively, if you break it up after it has congealed, and put it into a glass bowl, or heap it in jelly glasses Unless it is broken, its sparkling clearness shows to little advantage.

After the clear jelly has done dripping, you may return the ingredients to the kettle, and warm them over again for about five minutes. Then put them into the bag (which you may now squeeze hard) till all the liquid is pressed out of it into a second dish or bowl. This last jelly cannot, of course, be clear, but it will taste very well, and may be eaten in the family.

A pound of the best raisins picked and washed, and boiled with the other ingredients, is thought by many persons greatly to improve the richness and flavour or calves' feet jelly. They must be put in whole, and can be afterwards used for a pudding.

Similar jelly may be made of pigs' or sheep's feet; but it is not so nice and delicate as that of calves.

By boiling two sets, or eight calves' feet in five quarts of Water, you may be sure of having the jelly very firm. In damp weather it is sometimes very difficult to get it to congeal if you use but one set of feet; there is the same risk if the weather is hot. In winter it maybe made several days before it is to be eaten. In summer it will keep in ice for two days; perhaps longer.

TO PRESERVE CREAM.

Take four quarts of new cream; it must he of the richest quality, and have no milk mixed with it. Put it into a preserving kettle, and simmer it gently over the fire; carefully taking off whatever scum may rise to the top, till nothing more appears. Then stir, gradually, into it four pounds of double-refined loaf-sugar that has been finely powdered and sifted. Let the cream and sugar boil briskly together half an hour; skimming it, if necessary, and afterwards stirring it as long as it continues on the fire. Put it into small bottles; and when it is cold, cork it, and secure the corks with melted rosin. This cream, if properly prepared, will keep perfectly good during a long sea voyage.

ITALIAN CREAM.

Put two pints of cream into two bowls. With one bowl mix six ounces of powdered loaf-sugar, the juice of two large lemons, and two glasses of white wine. Then add the other pint of cream, and stir the whole very hard. Boil two ounces, of isinglass with, four small tea-cups full of water, till it is reduced to one half. Then stir the isinglass lukewarm, into the other ingredients, and put them into a glass dish to congeal.

CHOCOLATE CREAM.

Melt six ounces of scraped chocolate and four ounces of white sugar in half a pint of boiling; water. Stir in an ounce of dissolved isinglass. When the whole has boiled, pour it into a mould.

COLOURING FOR CONFECTIONARY.

RED.

Take twenty grains of cochineal, and fifteen grains of cream of tartar finely powdered; add to them a piece of alum the size of a cherry stone, and boil them with a jill of soft water, in an earthen vessel, slowly, for half an hour. Then strain it through muslin, and keep it tightly-corked in a phial.

COCHINEAL FOR PRESENT USE.

Take two cents' worth of cochineal. Lay it on a flat plate, and bruise it with the blade of a knife. Put it into half a tea-cup of white brandy. Let it stand a quarter of an hour, and then filter it through fine muslin.

YELLOW COLOURING.

Take a little saffron, put it into an earthen vessel with a very small quantity of cold soft water, and let it steep till the colour of the infusion is a bright yellow. Then strain it. The yellow seeds of lilies will answer nearly the saffron's purpose.

GREEN.

Take fresh spinach or beet leaves, and pound them in a marble mortar. If you want it for immediate use, take off the green froth as it rises, and mix it with the article you intend to colour. If you wish to keep it a few days, take the juice when you have pressed out a tea-cup full, and adding to it a piece of alum the size of a pea, give it a boil in a sauce-pan.

WHITE

Blanch some almonds, soak them in cold water, and then pound them to a smooth paste in a marble mortar; adding at intervals a little rose water. Thick cream will communicate a white colour.

These preparations may be used for jellies, ice creams, blanc-mange, syllabubs, icing for cakes; and for various articles of confectionary.

CAKES, ETC.

GENERAL OBSERVATIONS.

Unless you are provided with proper and convenient utensils and materials, the difficulty of preparing cakes will be great, and in most instances a failure; involving disappointment, waste of time, and useless expense. Accuracy in proportioning the ingredients is indispensable; and therefore scales and weights, and a set of tin measures (at least from a quart down to a jill) are of the utmost importance. A large sieve for flour is also necessary; and smaller ones for sugar and spice. There should be a marble mortar, or one of lignum vitae, (the hardest of all wood;) those of iron (however well, tinned) are apt to discolour the articles pounded in them. Spice may be ground in a mill kept, exclusively for that purpose. Every kitchen should be provided with spice-boxes. You should have a large grater for lemon, cocoa-nut, &c., and a small one for nutmeg. Butter and sugar cannot be stirred together conveniently without a spaddle or spattle, which is a round stick flattened at one end; and a deep earthen pan with sides nearly straight. For beating eggs, you should have hickory rods or a wire whip, and broad shallow earthen pans. Neither the eggs, nor the butter and sugar should be beaten, in tin, as the coldness of the metal will prevent them from becoming light.

For baking large cakes, the pans (whether of block tin or earthen) should have straight sides; if the aides slope inward, there will be much difficulty in icing the cake. Pans with a hollow tube going up from the centre, are supposed to diffuse the heat more equally through the middle of the cake. Buns and some other cakes should be baked in square shallow pans of block tin or iron. Little tins for queen cakes, &c. are most convenient when of a round or oval shape. All baking pans, whether large or small, should be well greased with butter or lard before the mixture is put into them, and should be filled but little more than half. You should have at least two dozen little tins, that a second supply may be ready for the oven, the moment the first is taken out. You will also want tin cutters for cakes that are rolled out in dough.

All the utensils should be cleaned and put away as soon as they are done with. They should be all kept together, and, if possible, not used for any other purposes. [Footnote: All the utensils necessary for cake and pastry-making, (and for the other branches of cooking,) may be purchased in Philadelphia; at Gideon Cox's household store in Market street, No. 335, two doors below Ninth. Every thing of the sort will be found there in great variety, of good quality, and at reasonable prices.]

As it is always desirable that, cake-making should be commenced at an early hour, it is well on the day previous to ascertain if all the materials are in the house; that there may be no unnecessary delay from sending or waiting for them in the morning. Wastefulness is to be avoided in every thing; but it is utterly impossible that cakes can be good (or indeed any thing else) without a liberal allowance of good materials. Cakes are frequently rendered hard, heavy, and uneatable by a misplaced economy in eggs and butter; or tasteless and insipid for want of their due seasoning of spice, lemon, &c.

Use no flour but the best superfine; if the flour is of inferior. quality, the cakes will he heavy, ill-coloured, and unfit to eat. Even the best flour should always be sifted. No butter that is not fresh and good; should ever be put into cakes; for it will give them a disagreeable taste which can never be disguised by the other ingredients. Even when of excellent quality, the butter will be improved by washing it in cold, water, and squeezing and pressing it. Except for gingerbread, use only white sugar, (for the finest cakes the best loaf,) and have it pulverized by pounding it in a mortar, or crushing it on the paste-board with the rolling-pin. It should then be sifted. In mixing butter and sugar, sift the sugar into a deep pan, cut up the butter in it, set it in a warm place to soften, and then stir it very hard with the spaddle, till it becomes quite light, and of the consistence of cream. In preparing eggs, break them one at a time, into a saucer, that, in case there should be a bad one among them, it may not spoil the others. Put them into a broad shallow pan, and beat them with rods or with a wire whisk, not merely till they froth, but long afterwards, till the froth subsides, and they become thick and smooth like boiled custard. White of egg by itself may be beaten with small rods, or with a three-pronged fork, or a broad knife. It is a very easy process, and should be continued till the liquid is all converted into a stiff froth so firm that it will not drop from the rods when held up. In damp weather it is sometimes difficult to get the froth stiff.

The first thing to be done in making cake, is to weigh or measure all the ingredients. Next sift the flour, powder the sugar, pound or grind the spice, and prepare the fruit; afterwards mix and stir the butter and sugar, and lastly beat the eggs; as, if allowed to stand any time, they will fall and become heavy. When all the ingredients are mixed together, they should be stirred very hard at the last; and (unless there is yeast in the cake) the sooner it is put into the oven the better. While baking, no air should be admitted to it, except for a moment, now and then, when it is necessary to examine if it is baking properly, For baking; cakes, the best guide is practice and experience; so much depending on the state of the fire, that it is impossible to lay down any infallible rules.

If you bake in a Dutch oven, let the lid be first heated by standing it up before the fire; and cover the inside of the bottom with sand or ashes, to temper the heat. For the same purpose, when you bake in a stove, place bricks under the pans. Sheets of iron without sides will be found very useful for baking small flat cakes. For cakes of this description, the fire should be brisk; if baked slowly, they will spread, lose their shape, and run into each other. For all cakes, the heat should be regular and even; if one part of the oven is cooler than another, the cake will bake imperfectly, and have heavy streaks through it. Gingerbread (on account of the molasses) is more apt to scorch and burn than any other cake; therefore it should he baked with a moderate fire.

It is safest, when practicable, to send all large cakes to a professional baker's; provided they can be put immediately into the oven, as standing will spoil them. If you bake them at home, you will find that they are generally done when they cease to make a simmering noise; and when on probing them to the bottom with a twig from a broom, or with the blade of the knife, it comes out quite clean. The fire should then be withdrawn, and the cake allowed to get cold in the oven. Small cakes should be laid to cool on an inverted sieve. It may be recommended to novices in the art of baking, to do every thing in little tins or in very shallow pans; there being then less risk than with a large thick cake. In mixing batter that is to be baked in small cakes; use less proportion of flour.

Small cakes should be kept closely covered in stone jars. For large ones, you should have broad stone pans with close lids, or else tin boxes. All cakes that are made with yeast should be eaten quite fresh; so also should sponge cake. Some sorts may be kept a week; black cake much longer.

BLACK CAKE.

Prepare two pounds of currants by picking them clean, washing and draining them, through a cullender, and then spreading them out on a large dish to dry before the fire or in the sun, placing the dish in a slanting position. Pick and stone two pounds of the best raisins, and cut them in half. Dredge the currants (when they are dry) and the raisins thickly with flour to prevent them from sinking in the cake. Grind or powder as much cinnamon as will make a large gravy-spoonful when done; also a table-spoonful of mace and four nutmegs; sift these spices, and mix them all together in a cup. Mix together two large glasses of white wine, one of brandy and one of rose water, and cut a pound of citron into large slips. Sift a pound of flour into one pan, and a pound of powdered loaf-sugar into another. Cut up among the sugar a pound of the best fresh butter, and stir them to a cream. Beat twelve eggs till perfectly thick and smooth, and stir them gradually into the butter and sugar, alternately with the flour. Then add by degrees, the fruit, spice and liquor, and stir the whole very hard at the last. Then put the mixture into a well-buttered tin pan with straight or perpendicular sides. Put it immediately into a moderate oven, and bake it at least four hours. When done, let it remain in the oven to get cold; it will be the better for staying in all night. Ice it next morning; first dredging the outside all over with flour, and then wiping it with a towel. This will make the icing stick.

ICING.

A quarter of a pound of finely powdered loaf-sugar, of the whitest and best quality, is the usual allowance to one white of egg. For the cake in the preceding receipt, three quarters of a pound of sugar and the whites of three eggs will be about the proper quantity. Beat the white of egg by itself till it stands alone. Have ready the powdered sugar, and then beat it hard into the white of egg, till it becomes thick and smooth; flavouring it as you proceed with a few drops of oil of lemon, or a little extract of roses. Spread it evenly over the cake with a broad knife or a feather; if you find it too thin, beat in a little more powdered sugar. Cover with it thickly the top and sides of the cake, taking care not to have it rough and streaky. To ice well requires skill and practice. When the icing is about half dry, put on the ornaments. You may flower it with coloured sugar-sand or nonparels; but a newer and more elegant mode is to decorate it with, devices and borders in white sugar; they can be procured at the confectioners, and look extremely well on icing that has been tinted with pink by the addition of a little cochineal.

You may colour icing of a pale or deep yellow, by rubbing the lumps of loaf-sugar (before they are powdered) upon the outside of a large lemon or orange. This will also flavour it finely.

Almond icing, for a very fine cake, is made by mixing gradually with the white of egg and. sugar, some almonds, half bitter and half sweet, that have been pounded in a mortar with rose water to a smooth paste. The whole must be well incorporated, and spread over the cake near half an inch thick. It must be set in a cool oven to dry, and then taken out and covered with a smooth plain icing of sugar and white of egg.

Whatever icing is left, may be used to make maccaroons or kisses.

POUND CAKE.

Prepare a table-spoonful of powdered cinnamon, a tea-spoonful of powdered mace, and two nutmegs grated or powdered. Mix together in a tumbler, a glass of white—wine, a glass of brandy, and a glass of rose water. Sift a pound of the finest flour into a broad pan, and powder a pound of loaf-sugar. Put the sugar into a deep pan, and cut up in it a pound of fresh butter. Warm them by the fire till soft; and then stir them to a cream. When they are perfectly light, add gradually the spice and liquor, a little at a time. Beat ten eggs as light as possible, and stir them by degrees into the mixture, alternately with the flour. Then add twelve drops of oil of lemon; or more, if it is not strong. Stir the whole very hard; put it into a deep tin pan with straight or upright sides, and bake it in a moderate oven from two to three hours. If baked in a Dutch oven, take off the lid when you have ascertained that the cake is quite done, and let it remain in the oven to cool gradually. If any part is burnt, scrape it off as soon as cold.

It may be iced either warm or cool; first dredging the cake with flour and then wiping it off. It will be best to put on two coats of icing; the second coat not till the first is entirely dry. Flavour the icing with essence of lemon, or with extract of roses.

This cake will be very delicate if made with a pound of rice flour instead of wheat.

INDIAN POUND CAKE.

Sift a pint of fine yellow Indian meal, and half a pint of wheat flour, and mix them well together. Prepare a nutmeg beaten, and mixed with a table-spoonful of powdered cinnamon. Stir together till very light, half a pound of powdered white sugar; and half a pound of fresh butter; adding the spice, with a glass of white wine, and a glass of brandy. Having beaten eight eggs as light as possible, stir them into the butter and sugar, a little at a time in turn with the meal. Give the whole a hard stirring at the last; put it into a well-buttered tin pan, and bake it about an hour and a half.

This cake (like every thing else in which Indian meal is an ingredient) should be eaten quite fresh; it is then very nice. When stale, (even a day old,) it becomes dry and rough as if made with saw-dust.

QUEEN CAKE.

Sift fourteen ounces of the finest flour, being two ounces less than a pound. Cakes baked in little tins, should have a smaller proportion of flour than those that are done in large loaves. Prepare a table-spoonful of beaten cinnamon, a tea-spoonful of mace, and two beaten nutmegs; and mix them all together when powdered. Mix in a tumbler, half a glass of white wine, half a glass of brandy, and half a glass of rose water. Powder a pound of loaf-sugar, and sift it into a deep pan; cut up in it a pound of fresh butter; warm them by the fire, and stir them to a cream. Add gradually the spice and the liquor. Beat ten eggs very light, and stir them into the mixture in turn with the flour. Stir in twelve drops of essence of lemon, and beat the whole very hard. Butter some little tins; half fill them with the mixture; set them into a brisk oven, and cake them about a quarter of an hour. When done, they will shrink from the sides of the tins. After you turn them out, spread them on an inverted sieve to cool. If you have occasion to fill your tins a second time, scrape and wipe them well before they are used again.

Make an icing flavoured with oil of lemon, or with extract of roses; and spread two coats of it on the queen cakes. Set them to dry in a warm place, but not near enough the fire to discolour the icing and cause it to crack.

Queen cakes are best the day they are baked.

FRUIT QUEEN CAKES.

Make them in the above manner, with the addition of a pound of currants, (picked, washed, dried, and floured,) and the juice and grated peel of two large lemons, stirred in gradually at the last. Instead of currants, you may put in sultana or seedless raisins, cut in half and floured.

You may make a fruit pound cake in this manner.

LADY CAKE.

Take a quarter of a pound of shelled bitter almonds, or peach-kernels. Put them into a bowl of boiling water, (renewing the water as it cools) and let them lie in it till the skin peels off easily; then throw them, as they, are blanched, into a bowl of cold water, which will much improve their whiteness. Pound them, one at a time, in a mortar; pouring in frequently a few drops of rose water to prevent them from oiling and being heavy. Cut up three quarters of a pound of fresh butter into a whole pound of powdered loaf-sugar. Having warmed it, stir it to a light cream, and then add very gradually the pounded almonds, beating them in very hard. Sift into a separate pan half a pound and two ounces of flour, and beat in another pan to a stiff froth, the, whites only of seventeen eggs. Stir the flour and the white of egg alternately into the pan of butter, sugar and almonds, a very little at a time of each. Having beaten the whole as hard as possible, put it into a buttered tin pan, (a square one is best,) and set it immediately into a moderate oven. Bake it about an hour, more or less, according to its thickness. When cool, ice it, flavouring the icing, with oil of lemon. It is best the day after it is baked, but it may be eaten fresh. When you put it away wrap it in a thick cloth.

If you bake it in little tins, use two ounces less of flour.

SPANISH BUNS.

Cut up three quarters of a pound of butter into a jill and a half or three wine glasses of rich unskimmed milk, (cream will be still better,) and get the pan on a stove or near the fire, till the butter becomes soft enough to stir all through the milk with a knife; but do not let it get so hot as to boil of itself. Then set it away in a cold place. Sift into separate pans, a half pound and a quarter of a pound of the finest flour; and having beaten four eggs as light as possible, mix them with the milk and butter, and then pour the whole into the pan that contains the half pound of flour. Having previously prepared two grated nutmegs, and a table-spoonful of powdered cinnamon and mace, stir them into the mixture; adding six drops of extract of roses, or a large table-spoonful of rose water. Add a wine glass and a half of the best fresh yeast from a brewery. If you cannot procure yeast of the very best quality, an attempt to make these buns will most probably prove a failure, as the variety of other ingredients will prevent them from rising unless the yeast is as strong as possible. Before you put it in, skim off the thin liquid or beer from the top, and then stir up the bottom. After you have put in the yeast, add the sugar; stirring it well in, a very little at a time. If too much sugar is put in at once, the buns will be heavy. Lastly, sprinkle in the quarter of a pound of flour that was sifted separately; and stir the whole very hard. Put the mixture into a square pan well buttered, and (having covered it with a cloth) place it in a corner of the hearth to rise, which will require, perhaps, about five hours; therefore these buns should always be made early in the day. Do not bake it till the batter has risen to twice its original quantity, and is covered on the top with bubbles; then set the pan into a moderate oven, and bake it about twenty minutes. Let it get cool in the pan; then, cut it into squares, and either ice them, (flavouring the icing with essence of lemon or extract of roses,) or sift grated loaf-sugar thickly over them. These buns (like all other cakes made with yeast) should be eaten the day they are baked; as when stale, they fall and become hard.

In mixing them, you may stir in at the last half a pound of raisins, stoned, chopped and floured; or half a pound of currants. If you use fruit, put in half a wine glass more of the yeast.

BATH BUNS.

Boil a little saffron in sufficient water to cover it, till the liquid is of a bright yellow; then strain it, and set it to cool. Rub half a pound of fresh butter into a pound of sifted flour, and make it into a paste with four eggs that have been well beaten, and a large wine glass of the best and strongest yeast; adding the infusion of saffron to colour it yellow. Put the dough into a pan, cover it with a cloth, and set it before the fire to rise. When it is quite light, mix into it a quarter of a pound of powdered and sifted loaf-sugar; a grated nutmeg; and, if you choose, two or three spoonfuls of carraway seeds. Roll out the dough into a thick sheet, and divide it into round cakes with a cutter. Strew the top of each bun with carraway comfits, and bake them on flat tins buttered well. They should be eaten the day they are baked, as they are not good unless quite fresh.

JELLY CAKE.

Sift three quarters of a pound of flour. Stir to a cream a pound of butter and a pound of powdered white sugar, and mix in half a tea-cup of rose water, and a grated nutmeg, with a tea-spoonful of powdered cinnamon. Beat ten eggs very light, and add them gradually to the mixture, alternately with the flour; stirring the whole very hard. Put your griddle into the oven of a stove; and when it is quite hot, grease it with fresh butter tied in a clean rag, and set on it a tin cake-ring, (about the size of a large dinner plate,) greased also. Dip out two large table-spoonfuls and a half of the cake batter; put it within the tin ring, and bake it about five minutes (or a little longer) without turning it. When it is done, take it carefully off; place it on a large dish to cool; wipe the griddle, grease it afresh, and put on another cake. Proceed thus till all the batter is baked. When the cakes are cool, spread every one thickly over with grape jelly, peach marmalade, or any other sweetmeat that is smooth and thick; currant jelly will be found too thin, and is liable to run off. Lay the cakes smoothly one on another, (each having a layer of jelly or marmalade between,) and either grate loaf-sugar over the top one, or ice it smoothly; marking the icing with cross lines of coloured sugar-sand, all the lines meeting at the centre so as to divide the cake, when cut, into triangular or wedge-shaped slices. If you ice it, add a few drops of essence of lemon to the icing.

Jelly cake should be eaten fresh. It is best the day it is baked.

You may bake small jelly cakes in muffin rings.

SPONGE CAKE.

Sift three quarters of a pound of flour, [Footnote: Sponge cake may be made with rice flour.] and powder a pound of the best loaf-sugar. Grate the yellow rind and squeeze into a saucer the juice of three lemons. Beat twelve eggs; and when they are as light as possible, beat into them gradually and very hard the sugar, adding the lemon, and beating the whole for a long time. Then by degrees, stir in the flour slowly and lightly; for if the flour is stirred hard and fast into sponge cake, it will make it porous and tough. Have ready buttered, a sufficient number of little square tins, (the thinner they are the better,) half fill them with the mixture; grate loaf-sugar over the top of each; put them immediately into a quick oven, and bake them about ten minutes; taking out one to try when you think they are done. Spread them on an inverted sieve to cool. When baked in small square cakes, they are generally called Naples biscuits.

If you are willing to take the trouble, they will bake much nicer in little square paper cases, which you must make of a thick letter paper, turning up the sides all round, and pasting together or sewing up the corners.

If you bake the mixture in one large cake, (which is not advisable unless you have had much practice in baking,) put it into a buttered tin pan or mould, and set it directly into a hot Dutch oven, as it will fall and become heavy if allowed to stand. Keep plenty of live coals on the top, and under the bottom till the cake has risen very high, and is of a fine colour; then diminish the fire, and keep it moderate till the cake is done. It will take about an hour. When cool, ice it; adding a little essence of lemon or extract of roses to the icing. Sponge cake is best the day it is baked.

Diet Bread is another name for Sponge Cake.

ALMOND CAKE.

Blanch, and pound in a mortar, four ounces of shelled sweet almonds and two ounces of shelled bitter ones; adding, as you proceed, sufficient rose-water to make them light and white. Sift half a pound of flour, and powder a pound of loaf-sugar. Beat thirteen eggs; and when they are as light as possible, stir into them alternately the almonds, sugar, and flour; adding a grated nutmeg. Butter a large square pan; put in the mixture, and bake it in a brisk oven about half an hour, less or more, according to its thickness. When cool, ice it. It is best when eaten fresh.

COCOA-NUT CAKE.

Cut up and wash a cocoa-nut, and grate as much of it as will weigh a pound. Powder a pound of loaf-sugar. Beat fifteen eggs very light; and then beat into them, gradually, the sugar. Then add by degrees the cocoa-nut; and lastly, a handful of sifted flour. Stir the whole very hard, and bake it either in a large tin pan, or in little tins. The oven should be rather quick.

WASHINGTON CAKE.

Stir together a pound of butter and a pound of sugar; and sift into another pan a pound of flour. Beat six eggs very light, and stir them into the butter and sugar, alternately with the flour and a pint of rich milk or cream; if the milk is sour it will be no disadvantage. Add a glass of wine, a glass of brandy, a powdered nutmeg, and a table-spoonful of powdered cinnamon. Lastly, stir in a small tea-spoonful of pearl-ash, or salaeratus, that has been melted in a little vinegar; take care not to put in too much pearl-ash, lest it give the cake an unpleasant taste. Stir the whole very hard; put it into a buttered tin pan, (or into little tins,) and bake it in a brisk oven. Wrapped in a thick cloth, this cake will keep soft for a week.

CIDER CAKE.

Pick, wash, and dry a pound of currants, and sprinkle them well with flour; and prepare two nutmegs, and a large table-spoonful of powdered cinnamon. Sift half a pound and two ounces of flour. Stir together till very light. six ounces of fresh butter, and half a pound of powdered white sugar; and add gradually the spice, with two wine glasses of brandy, (or one of brandy and one of white wine.) Beat four eggs very light, and stir them into the mixture alternately with the flour. Add by degrees half a pint of brisk cider; and then stir in the currants, a few at a time. Lastly, a small tea-spoonful of pearl-ash or sal-aratus dissolved in a little warm water. Having stirred the whole very hard, put it into a buttered tin pan, and let it stand before the fire half an hour previous to baking. Bake it in a brisk oven an hour or more according to its thickness. Or you may bake it as little cakes, putting it into small tins; in which case use but half a pound of flour in raising the batter.

ELECTION CAKE.

Make a sponge (as it is called) in the following manner:—Sift into a pan two pounds and a half of flour; and into a deep plate another pound. Take a second pan, and stir a large table-spoonful of the best West India molasses into five jills or two tumblers and a half of strong fresh yeast; adding a jill of water, warm, but not hot. Then stir gradually into the yeast, &c. the pound of flour that you have sifted separately. Cover it, and let it set by the fire three hours to rise. While it is rising, prepare the other ingredients, by stirring in a deep pan two pounds of fresh butter and two pounds of powdered sugar, till they are quite light and creamy; adding to them a table-spoonful of powdered cinnamon; a tea-spoonful of powdered mace; and two powdered nutmegs. Stir in also half a pint of rich milk. Beat fourteen eggs till very smooth and thick, and stir them gradually into the mixture, alternately with the two pounds and a half of flour which you sifted first. When the sponge is quite light, mix the whole together, and bake it in buttered tin pans in a moderate oven. It should be eaten fresh, as no sweet cake made with yeast is so good after the first day. If it is not probable that the whole will come into use on the day it is baked, mix but half the above quantity.

MORAVIAN SUGAR CAKE.

Cut up a quarter of a pound of butter into a pint of rich milk, and warm it till the butter becomes soft; then stir it about in the milk so as to mix them well. Sift three quarters of a pound of flour (or a pint and a half) into a deep pan, and making a hole in the middle of it, stir in a large table-spoonful of the best brewer's yeast in which a salt-spoonful of salt has been dissolved; and then thin it with the milk and butter. Cover it, and set it near the fire to rise. If the yeast is sufficiently strong, it will most probably be light in two hours. When it is quite light, mix with the dough a well-beaten egg and three quarters of a pound more of sifted flour; adding a table-spoonful of powdered cinnamon, and stirring it very hard. Butter a deep square baking pan, and put the mixture into it. Set it to rise again, as before. Mix together five ounces or a large coffee-cup of fine brown sugar; two ounces of butter; and two table-spoonfuls of powdered cinnamon. When the dough is thoroughly light, make deep incisions all over it, at equal distances, and fill them with the mixture of butter, sugar and cinnamon; pressing it hard down into the bottom of the holes, and closing the dough a little at the top to prevent the seasoning from running out. Strew some sugar over the top of the cake; set it immediately into the oven, and bake it from twenty minutes to half an hour, or more, in a brisk oven, in proportion to its thickness. When cool, cut it into squares. This is a very good plain cake; but do not attempt it unless you have excellent yeast.

HUCKLEBERRY CAKE.

Spread a quart of ripe huckleberries on a large dish, and dredge them thickly with flour. Mix together half a pint of milk; half a pint of molasses; half a pint of powdered sugar; and half a pound of butter. Warm them by the fire till the butter is quite soft; then stir them all together, and set them away till cold. Prepare a large table-spoonful of powdered cloves and cinnamon mixed. Beat five eggs very light, and stir them gradually into the other ingredients; adding, by degrees, sufficient gifted flour to make a thick batter. Then stir in a small tea-spoonful of pearl-ash or dissolved sal-aratus. Lastly, add by degrees the huckleberries. Put the mixture into a buttered pan, or into little tins and bake it in a moderate oven. It is best the second day.

BREAD CAKE.

When you are making wheat bread, and the dough is quite light and ready to bake, take out as much of it as would make a twelve cent loaf, and mix with it a tea cup full of powdered sugar, and a tea-cup full of butter that has been softened and stirred about in a tea-cup of warm milk. Add also a beaten egg. Knead it very well, put it into a square pan, dredged with flour, cover it, and set it near the fire for half an hour. Then bake it in a moderate oven, and wrap it in a thick cloth as soon as it is done. It is best when fresh.

FEDERAL CAKES.

Sift two pounds of flour into a deep pan, and cut up in it a pound of fresh butter; rub the butter into the flour with your hands, adding by degrees, half a pound of powdered white sugar; a tea-spoonful of powdered cinnamon; a beaten nutmeg; a glass of wine or brandy, and two glasses of rose water. Beat four eggs very light; and add them to the mixture with a salt-spoonful of pearl-ash melted in a little lukewarm water. Mix all well together; add, if necessary, sufficient cold water to make it into a dough just stiff enough to roll out; knead it slightly, and then roll it out into a sheet about half an inch thick. Cut it out into small cakes with a tin cutter, or with the edge of a tumbler; dipping the cutter frequently into flour, to prevent its sticking. Lay the cakes in shallow pans buttered, or on flat sheets of tin, (taking care not to let them touch, lest they should run into each other,) and bake them of a light brown in a brisk oven. They are best the second day.

SAVOY BISCUITS.

Take four eggs, and separate the whites from the yolks. Beat the whites by themselves, to a stiff froth; then add gradually the yolks, and beat them both together for a long time. Next add by degrees half a pound of the finest loaf-sugar, powdered and sifted, beating it in very hard; and eight drops of strong essence of lemon. Lastly, stir in a quarter of a pound of sifted flour, a little at a time. Stir the whole very hard, and then with a spoon lay it on sheets of white paper, forming it into thin cakes of an oblong or oval shape. Take care not to place them too close to each other, lest they run. Grate loaf-sugar over the top of each, to assist in keeping them in shape. Have the oven quite ready to put them in immediately. It should be rather brisk. They will bake in a few minutes, and should be but slightly coloured.

ALMOND MACCAROONS.

Take a pound of shelled sweet almonds, and a quarter of a pound of shelled bitter almonds. Blanch them in scalding water, mix them together, and pound them, one or two at a time, in a mortar to a very smooth paste; adding frequently a little rose water to prevent them from oiling and becoming heavy. Prepare a pound of powdered loaf-sugar. Beat the whites of seven eggs, to a stiff froth, and then beat into it gradually the powdered sugar, adding a table-spoonful of mixed spice, (nutmeg, mace, and cinnamon.) Then mix in the pounded almonds, (which it is best to prepare the day before,) and stir the whole very hard. Form the mixture with a spoon into little round or oval cakes, upon sheets of buttered white paper, and grate white sugar over each. Lay the paper in square shallow pans, or on iron sheets, and bake the maccaroons a few minutes in a brisk oven, till of a pale brown. When cold, take them off the papers.

It will be well to try two or three first, and if you find them likely to lose their shape and run info each other, you may omit the papers and make the mixture up into little balls with your hands well floured; baking them in shallow tin pans slightly buttered.

You may make maccaroons with icing that is left from a cake.

COCOA-NUT MACCAROONS.

Beat to a stiff froth the whites of six eggs, and then beat into it very hard a pound of powdered loaf-sugar. Mix with it a pound of grated cocoa-nut, or sufficient to make a stiff paste. Then flour your hands, and make it up into little balls. Lay them on sheets of buttered white paper, and bake them in a brisk oven; first grating loaf-sugar over each. They will be done in a few minutes. Maccaroons may be made in a similar manner of pounded cream-nuts, ground-nuts, filberts, or English walnuts.

WHITE COCOA-NUT CAKES.

Break up a cocoa-nut; peel and wash the pieces in cold water, and grate them. Mix in the milk of the nut and some powdered loaf-sugar and then form the grated cocoa-nut into little balls upon sheets of white paper. Make them all of a regular and handsome form, and touch the top of each with a spot of red sugar-sand. Do not bake them, but place them to dry for twenty-four hours, in a warm room where nothing is likely to disturb the them.

COCOA-NUT JUMBLES.

Grate a large cocoa-nut. Rub half a pound of butter into a pound of sifted flour, and wet it with, three beaten eggs, and a little rose water. Add by degrees the cocoa-nut, so as to form a stiff dough. Flour your hands and your paste-hoard, and dividing the dough into equal portions, make the jumbles with your hands into long rolls, and then curl them round and join the ends so as to form rings. Grate loaf-sugar over them, lay them in buttered pans, (not so near as to run into each other,) and bake them in a quick oven from five to ten minutes.

COMMON JUMBLES.

Sift a pound of flour into a large pan. Cut up a pound of butter into a pound of powdered white sugar, and stir them to a cream. Beat six eggs till very light, and then pour them all at once into the pan of flour; next add the butter and sugar, with a large table-spoonful of mixed mace and cinnamon, two grated nutmegs, and a tea-spoonful of essence of lemon or a wine glass of rose water. When all the ingredients are in, stir the mixture very hard with a broad knife. Having floured your hands and spread some flour on the paste-board, make the dough into long rolls, (all of equal size,) and form them into rings by joining the two ends very nicely. Lay them on buttered tins, and bake them in a quick oven from five to ten minutes. Grate sugar over them when cool.

APEES.

Rub a pound of fresh butter into two pounds of sifted flour, and mix in a pound of powdered white sugar, a grated nutmeg, a table-spoonful of powdered cinnamon, and four large table-spoonfuls of carraway seeds. Add a wine glass of rose water, and mix the whole with sufficient cold water to make it a stiff dough. Roll it out into a large sheet about a third of an inch in thickness, and cut it into round cakes with a tin cutter or with the edge of a tumbler. Lay them in buttered pans, and bake them in a quick oven, (rather hotter at the bottom than at the top,) till they are of a very pale brown.

WHITE CUP CAKE.

Measure one large coffee cup of cream or rich milk, (which, for this cake, is best when sour,) one cup of fresh butter; two cups of powdered white sugar; and four cups of sifted flour. Stir the butter and sugar together till quite light; then by degrees add the cream, alternately with half the flour. Beat five eggs as light as possible, and stir them into the mixture, alternately with the remainder of the flour. Add a grated nutmeg and a large tea-spoonful of powdered cinnamon, with eight drops of oil of lemon. Lastly, stir in a very small tea-spoonful of sal-aratus or pearl-ash, melted in a little vinegar or lukewarm water. Having stirred the whole very hard, put it into little tins; set them in a moderate oven, and bake them about twenty minutes.

KISSES.

Powder a pound of the best loaf-sugar. Beat to a strong froth the whites of eight eggs, and when it is stiff enough to stand alone, beat into it the powdered sugar, (a tea spoonful at a time,) adding the juice of two lemons, or ten drops of essence of lemon. Having beaten the whole very hard, drop it in oval or egg-shaped heaps upon sheets of white paper, smoothing them with the spoon and making them of a handsome and regular form. Place them in a moderate oven, (if it is too cool they will not rise, but will flatten and run into each other,) and bake them till coloured of a very pale brown. Then take them off the papers very carefully, place two bottoms (or flat sides) together, so as to unite them in an oval ball, and lay them on their sides to cool. To manage them properly, requires so much practice and dexterity, that it is best, when practicable, to procure kisses from a confectioner's shop.

MARMALADE CAKE.

Make a batter as for queen-cake, and bake it in small tin rings on a griddle. Beat white of egg, and powdered loaf-sugar according to the preceding receipt, flavouring it with lemon. When the batter is baked into cakes, and they are quite cool, spread over each a thick layer of marmalade, and then heap on with a spoon tire icing or white of egg and sugar. Pile it high, and set the cakes in a moderate oven till the icing is coloured of a very pale brown.

Instead of small ones you may bake the whole in one large cake.

SECRETS.

Take glazed paper of different colours, and cut it into squares of equal size, fringing two sides of each. Have ready, burnt almonds, chocolate nuts, and bonbons or sugar-plums of various sorts; and put one in each paper with a folded slip containing two lines of verse; or what will be much more amusing, a conundrum with the answer. Twist the coloured paper so as entirely to conceal their contents, leaving the fringe at each end. This is the most easy, but there are various ways of cutting and ornamenting these envelopes.

SCOTCH CAKE.

Rub three quarters of a pound of butter into a pound of sifted flour; mix in a pound of powdered sugar, and a large table-spoonful of powdered cinnamon. Mix it into a dough with three well beaten eggs. Roll it out into a sheet; cut it into round cakes, and bake them in a quick oven; they will require but a few minutes.

SCOTCH QUEEN CAKE.

Melt a pound of butter by putting it into a skillet on hot coals. Then set it away to cool. Sift a quarter of a peck of flour into a deep pan, and mix with it a pound of powdered sugar and a table-spoonful of powdered cinnamon and mace. Make a hole in the middle, put in the melted butter, and mix it with a knife till you have formed of the whole a lump of dough. If it is too stiff, moisten it with a little rose water. Do not knead it; but roll it out into a large oval sheet, an inch thick. Cut it down the middle, and then across, so as to divide it into four cakes. Prick them with a fork, and crimp or scollop the edges neatly. Lay them in shallow pans; set them, in a quick oven and bake them of a light brown. This cake will keep a week or two.

You may mix in with the dough half a pound of currants, picked, washed, and dried.

HONEY CAKES.

Take a quart of strained honey, half a pound of fresh butter, and a small tea-spoonful of pearl-ash dissolved in a wine glass of water. Add by degrees as much sifted flour as will make a stiff paste. Work the whole well together. Roll it out about half an inch thick. Cut it into cakes with the edge of a tumbler or with a tin-cake cutter. Lay them on buttered tins and bake them with rather a brisk fire, but see that they do not burn.

WAFER CAKES.

Mix together half a pound of powdered sugar, and a quarter of a pound of butter; and add to them six beaten eggs. Then beat the whole very light; stirring into it as much sifted flour as will make a stiff batter; a powdered nutmeg, and a tea-spoonful of cinnamon; and eight drops of oil of lemon, or a table-spoonful of rose water. The batter must be very smooth when it is done, and without a single lump. Heat your wafer iron on both sides by turning it in the fire; but do not allow it to get too hot. Grease the inside with butter tied in a rag, (this must be repeated previous to the baking of every cake,) and put in the batter, allowing to each wafer two large tablespoonfuls, taking care not to stir up the batter. Close the iron, and when one side is baked, turn it on the other; open it occasionally to see if the wafer is doing well. They should be coloured of a light brown. Take them out carefully with a knife. Strew them with powdered sugar, and roll them up while warm, round a smooth stick, withdrawing it when they grow cold. They are best the day after they are baked.

If you are preparing for company, fill up the hollow of the wafers with whipt cream, and stop up the two ends with preserved strawberries, or with any other small sweetmeat.

WONDERS, OR CRULLERS.

Rub half a pound of butter into two pounds of sifted flour, mixing in three quarters of a pound of powdered sugar. Add a tea-spoonful of powdered cinnamon, and a grated nutmeg, with a large table-spoonful of rose water. Beat six eggs very light, and stir them into the mixture. Mix it with a knife into a soft paste. Then put it on the paste-board, and roll it out into a sheet an inch thick. If you find it too soft, knead in a little more flour, and roll it out over again. Cut it into long slips with a jagging iron, or with a sharp knife, and twist them into various fantastic shapes. Have ready on hot coals, a skillet of boiling lard; put in the crullers and fry them of a light brown, turning them occasionally by means of a knife and fork. Take them out one by one on a perforated skimmer, that the lard may drain off through the holes. Spread them out on a large dish, and when cold grate white sugar over them.

They will keep a week or more.

DOUGH NUTS.

Take two deep dishes, and sift three quarters of a pound of flour into each. Make a hole in the centre of one of them, and pour in a wine glass of the best brewer's yeast; mix the flour gradually into it, wetting it with lukewarm milk; cover it, and set it by the fire to rise for about two hours.

This is setting a sponge. In the mean time, cut up five ounces of butter into the other dish of flour, and rub it fine with your hands; add half a pound of powdered sugar, a tea-spoonful of powdered cinnamon, a grated nutmeg, a table-spoonful of rose water, and a half pint of milk. Beat three eggs very light, and stir them hard into the mixture. Then when, the sponge is perfectly light, add it to the other ingredients, mixing them all thoroughly with a knife. Cover it, and set it again by the fire for another hour. When, it is quite light, flour your paste-board, turn out the lump of dough, and cut it into thick diamond shaped cakes with a jagging iron. If you find the dough so soft as to be unmanageable, mix in a little more flour; but not else. Have ready a skillet of boiling lard; put the dough-nuts into it, and fry them brown; and when cool grate loaf-sugar over them. They should be eaten quite fresh, as next day they will be tough and heavy; therefore it is best to make no more than you want for immediate use. The New York Oley Koeks are dough-nuts with currants and raisins in them.

WAFFLES.

Put two pints of rich milk into separate pans. Cut up and melt in one of them a quarter of a pound of butter, warming it slightly; then, when it is melted, stir it about, and set it away to cool. Beat eight eggs till very light, and mix them gradually into the other pan of milk, alternately with half a pound of flour. Then mix in by degrees the milk that has the butter in it. Lastly, stir in a large table-spoonful of strong fresh yeast. Cover the pan, and set it near the fire to rise. When the batter is quite light, heat your waffle-iron, by putting it among the coals of a clear bright fire; grease the inside with butter tied in a rag, and then put in some batter. Shut the iron closely, and when the waffle is done on one side, turn the iron on the other. Take the cake out by slipping a knife underneath; and then heat and grease the iron for another waffle. Send them to table quite hot, four or six on a plate; having buttered them and strewed over each a mixture of powdered cinnamon, and white sugar. Or you may send the sugar and cinnamon in a little glass bowl.

In buying waffle-irons, do not choose those broad shallow ones that are to hold four at a time; as the waffles baked in them are too small, too thin, and are never of a good shape. The common sort that bake but two at once are much the best.

NEW YORK COOKIES.

Take a half-pint or a tumbler full of cold water, and mix it with half a pound of powdered white sugar. Sift three pounds of flour into a large pan and cut up in it a pound of butter; rub the butter very fine into the flour. Add a grated nutmeg, and a tea-spoonful of powdered cinnamon, with a wine glass of rose water. Work in the sugar, and make the whole into a stiff dough, adding, if necessary, a little cold water. Dissolve a tea-spoonful of pearl-ash in just enough of warm water to cover it, and mix it in at the last. Take the lump of dough out of the pan, and knead it on the paste-board till it becomes quite light. Then roll it out rather more than half an inch thick, and cut it into square cakes with a jagging iron or with a sharp knife. Stamp the surface of each with a cake print. Lay them in buttered pans, and bake them of a light brown in a brisk oven.

They are similar to what are called New Year's cakes, and will keep two or three weeks.

In mixing the dough, you may add three table-spoonfuls of carraway seeds.

SUGAR BISCUIT.

Wet a pound of sugar with two large tea-cups full of milk; and rub a pound of butter into two pounds of flour; adding a table-spoonful of cinnamon, and a handful of carraway seeds. Mix in the sugar, add a tea-spoonful of pearl-ash dissolved, and make the whole into a stiff dough. Knead it, and then roll it out into a sheet about half an inch thick. Beat it on both sides with the rolling-pin, and then cut it out with the edge of a tumbler into round cakes. Prick them with a fork, lay them in buttered pans, and bake them light brown in a quick oven. You may colour them yellow by mixing in with the other ingredients a little of the infusion of saffron.

RUSKS.

Sift three pounds of flour into a large pan, and rub into it half a pound of butter, and half a pound of sugar. Beat two eggs very light, and stir them into a pint and a half of milk, adding two table-spoonfuls of rose water, and three table-spoonfuls of the best and strongest yeast. Make a hole in the middle of the flour, pour in the liquid, and gradually mix the flour into it till you have a thick batter. Cover it, and set it by the fire to rise. When it is quite light, put it on your paste-board and knead it well. Then divide it into small round cakes and knead each separately. Lay them very near each other in shallow iron pans that have been sprinkled with flour. Prick the top of each rusk with a fork, and set them by the fire to rise again for half an hour or more. When they are perfectly light, bake them in a moderate oven. They are best when fresh.

You can convert them into what are called Hard Rusks, or Tops and Bottoms, by splitting them in half, and putting them again into the oven to harden and crisp.

MILK BISCUIT.

Cut up three quarters of a pound of butter in a quart of milk, and set it near the fire to warm, till the butter becomes soft; then with a knife, mix it thoroughly with the milk, and set it away to cool. Afterwards stir in two wine glasses of strong fresh yeast, and add by degrees as much sifted flour as will make a dough just stiff enough to roll out. As soon as it is mixed, roll it into a thick sheet, and cut it out into round cakes with the edge of a tumbler or a wine glass. Sprinkle a large iron pan with flour; lay the biscuits in it, cover it and set it to rise near the fire. When the biscuits are quite light, knead each one separately; prick them with a fork, and set them again in a warm place for about half an hour. When they are light again, bake them in a moderate oven. They should be eaten fresh, and pulled open with the fingers, as splitting them with a knife will make them heavy.

WHITE GINGERBREAD.

Sift two pounds of flour into a deep pan, and rub into it three quarters of a pound of butter; then mix in a pound of common white sugar powdered; and three table-spoonfuls of the best white ginger. Having beaten four eggs very light, mix them gradually with the other ingredients in the pan, and add a small tea-spoonful of pearl-ash melted in a wine glass of warm milk. Stir the whole as hard as possible. Flour your paste-board; lay the lump of dough upon it, and roll it out into a sheet an inch thick; adding more flour if necessary. Butter a large shallow square pan. Lay the dough into it, and bake it in a moderate oven. When cold, cut it into squares. Or you may cut it out into separate cakes with a jagging iron, previous to baking. You must be careful not to lay them too close together in the pan, lest they run into each other.

COMMON GINGERBREAD.

Cut up a pound of butter in a quart of West India molasses, which must be perfectly sweet; if it is in the least sour, use sugar house molasses instead. Warm it slightly, just enough to melt the butter. Crush with the rolling-pin, on the paste-board, half a pound of brown sugar, and add it by degrees to the molasses and butter; then stir in a tea-cup full of powdered ginger, a large tea-spoonful of powdered cloves, and a table-spoonful of powdered cinnamon. Add gradually sufficient flour to make a dough stiff enough to roll out easily; and lastly, a small tea-spoonful of pearl-ash melted in a little warm water. Mix and stir the dough very hard with a spaddle, or a wooden spoon; but do not knead it. Then divide it with a knife into equal portions; and, having floured your hands, roll it out on the paste-board into long even strips. Place them in shallow tin pans, that have been buttered; either laying the strips side by side in straight round sticks, (uniting them at both ends,) or coil them into rings one within another, as you see them at the cake shops. Bake them in a brisk oven, taking care that they do not burn; gingerbread scorching sooner than any other cake.

To save time and trouble, you may roll out the dough into a sheet near an inch thick, and cut it into round flat cakes with a tin cutter, or with the edge of a tumbler.

Ground ginger loses much of its strength by keeping. Therefore it will be frequently found necessary to put in more than the quantity given in the receipt.

GINGERBREAD NUTS.

Rub half a pound of butter into a pound and a half of sifted flour; and mix in half a pound of brown sugar, crushed fine with the rolling-pin. Add two large table-spoonfuls of ginger, a tea-spoonful of powdered cloves, and a tea-spoonful of powdered cinnamon. Stir in a pint of molasses, and the grated peel of a large lemon, but not the juice, as you must add at the last, a very small tea-spoonful of pearl-ash dissolved in a little lukewarm water, and pearl-ash entirely destroys the taste of lemon-juice and of every other acid. Stir the whole mixture very hard with a spaddle or with a wooden spoon, and make it into a lump of dough just stiff enough to roll out into a sheet about half an inch thick. Cut it out into small cakes about the size of a quarter dollar; or make it up, with your hands well floured, into little round balls, flattening them on the top. Lay them in buttered pans, and bake them in a moderate oven. They will keep several weeks.

FRANKLIN CAKE.

Mix together a pint of molasses, and half a pint of milk, and cut up in it half a pound of butter. Warm them just enough to melt the butter, and then stir in six ounces of brown sugar; adding three table-spoonfuls of ginger, a table-spoonful of powdered cinnamon, a tea-spoonful of powdered cloves, and a grated nutmeg. Beat seven eggs very light, and stir them gradually into the mixture, in turn with a pound and two ounces of flour. Add, at the last, the grated peel and juice of two large lemons or oranges; or twelve drops of essence of lemon, there being no pearl-ash in this gingerbread. Stir the mixture very hard; put it into little queen cake tins, well buttered; and bake it in a moderate oven. It is best the second day, and will keep soft a week.

GINGER PLUM CAKE.

Stone a pound and a half of raisins, and cut them in two. Wash and dry half a pound of currants. Sift into a pan two pounds of flour. Put into another pan a pound of brown sugar, (rolled fine,) and cut up in it a pound of fresh butter. Stir the butter and sugar to a cream, and add to it two table-spoonfuls of the best ginger; one table-spoonful of powdered cinnamon; and one of powdered cloves. Then beat six eggs very light, and add them gradually to the butter and sugar, in turn with the flour and a quart of molasses. Lastly, stir in a tea-spoonful of pearl-ash dissolved in a little vinegar, and add by degrees the fruit, which must be well dredged with flour. Stir all very hard; put the mixture into a buttered pan, and bake it in a moderate oven. Take care not to let it burn.

MOLASSES CANDY.

Mix a pound of the best brown sugar with two quarts of West India molasses, (which must be perfectly sweet,) and boil it in a preserving kettle over a moderate fire for three hours, skimming it well, and stirring it frequently after the scum has ceased to rise; taking care that it does not burn. Have ready the grated rind and the juice of three lemons, and stir them into the molasses after it has boiled about two hours and a half; or you may substitute a large tea-spoonful of strong essence of lemon. The flavour of the lemon will all be boiled out if it is put in too soon. The mixture should boil at least three hours, that it may be crisp and brittle when cold. If it is taken off the fire too soon, or before it has boiled sufficiently, it will not congeal, but will be tough and ropy, and must be boiled over again. It will cease boiling of itself when it is thoroughly done. Then take it off the fire; have ready a square tin pan; put the mixture into it, and set it away to cool.

You may make molasses candy with almonds blanched and slit into pieces; stir them in by degrees after the mixture has boiled two hours and a half. Or you may blanch a quart of ground-nuts and put them in instead of the almonds.

NOUGAT.

Blanch a pound of shelled sweet almonds; and with an almond cutter, or a sharp penknife, split each almond into five slips. Spread them over a large dish, and place them in a gentle oven. Powder a pound of the finest loaf-sugar, and put it into a preserving pan without a drop of water. Set it on a chafing-dish over a slow fire, or on a hot stove, and stir it with a wooden spoon till the boat has entirely dissolved it. Then take the almonds out of the oven, and mix with them the juice of two or three lemons. Put them into the sugar a few at a time, and let them simmer till it becomes a thick stiff paste, stirring it hard all the while. Have ready a mould, or a square tin pan, greased all over the inside with sweet oil; put the mixture into it; smooth it evenly, and set it in a cold place to harden.

LEMON DROPS.

Squeeze some lemon-juice into a pan. Pound in a mortar some of the best loaf-sugar, and then sift it through a very fine sieve. Mix it with the lemon-juice, making it so thick that you can scarcely stir it. Put it into a porcelain sauce-pan, set it on hot coals, and stir it with a wooden spoon five minutes or more. Then take off the pan, and with the point of a knife drop the liquid on writing paper. When cold, the drops will easily come off.

Peppermint drops may be made as above, substituting for the lemon-juice essence of peppermint.

WARM CAKES FOR BREAKFAST AND TEA.

BUCKWHEAT CAKES.

Take a quart of buckwheat meal, mix with it a tea-spoonful of salt, and add a handful of Indian meal. Pour a large table-spoonful of the best brewer's yeast into the centre of the meal. Then mix it gradually with cold water till it becomes a batter. Cover it, put it in a warm place and set it to rise; it will take about three hours. When it is quite light, and covered with bubbles, it is fit to bake. Put your griddle over the fire, and let it get quite hot before you begin. Grease it well with a piece of butter tied in a rag. Then dip out a large ladle full of the batter and bake it on the griddle; turning it with a broad wooden paddle. Let the cakes be of large size, and even at the edges. Ragged edges to batter cakes look very badly. Butter them as you take them off the griddle. Put several on a plate, and cut them across in six pieces.

Grease the griddle anew, between baking each cake.

If your batter has been mixed over night and is found to be sour in the morning, melt in warm water a piece of pearl-ash the size of a grain of corn, or a little larger; stir it into the batter; let it set half an hour, and then bake it. The pearl-ash will remove the sour taste, and increase the lightness of the cakes.

FLANNEL CAKES.

Put a table-spoonful of butter into a quart of milk, and warm them together till the butter has melted; then stir it well, and set it away to cool. Beat five eggs as light as possible, and stir them into the milk in turn with three pints of sifted flour; add a small tea-spoonful of salt, and a large table-spoonful and a half of the best fresh yeast. Set the pan of batter near the fire to rise; and if the yeast is good, it will be light in three hours. Then bake it on a griddle in the manner of buckwheat cakes. Send them to table hot, and cut across into four pieces. This batter may be baked in waffle-irons. If so, send to table with the cakes powdered white sugar and cinnamon.

INDIAN BATTER CAKES.

Mix together a quart of sifted Indian meal, (the yellow meal is best for all purposes,) and a handful of wheat flour. Warm a quart of milk, and stir into it a small tea-spoonful of salt, and two large table-spoonfuls of the best fresh yeast. Beat three eggs very light, and stir them gradually into the milk in turn with the meal. Cover it, and set it to rise for three or four hours. When quite light, bake it on a griddle in the manner of buckwheat cakes. Butter them, cut them across, and send them to table hot, with molasses in a sauce-boat.

If the batter should chance to become sour before it is baked, stir in about a salt-spoonful of pearl-ash dissolved in a little lukewarm water; and let it set half an hour longer before it is baked.

INDIAN MUSH CAKES.

Pour into a pan three pints of cold water, and stir gradually into it a quart of sifted Indian meal which has been mixed with half a pint of wheat flour, and a small tea-spoonful of salt. Give it a hard stirring at the last. Have ready a hot griddle, and bake the batter immediately, in cakes about the size of a saucer. Send them to table piled evenly, but not cut. Eat them with butter or molasses.

This is the most economical and expeditious way of making soft Indian cakes; but it cannot be recommended as the best. It will be some improvement to mix the meal with milk rather than water.

JOHNNY CAKE.

Sift a quart of Indian meal into a pan; make a hole in the middle, and pour in a pint of warm water. Mix the meal and water gradually into a batter, adding a small tea-spoonful of salt. Beat it very hard, and for a long time, till it becomes quite light. Then spread it thick and even on a stout piece of smooth board. Place it upright on the hearth before a clear fire, with a flat iron or something of the sort to support the board behind, and bake it well. Cut it into squares, and split and butter them hot.

INDIAN FLAPPERS.

Have ready a pint of sifted Indian meal, mixed with a handful of wheat flour, and a small tea-spoonful of salt. Beat four eggs very light, and stir them by degrees into a quart of milk, in turn with the meal. They can be made in a very short time, and should be baked as soon as mixed, on a hot griddle; allow a large ladle full of batter to each cake, and make them all of the same size. Send them to table hot, buttered and cut in half.

INDIAN MUFFINS.

Sift and mix together a pint and a half of yellow Indian meal, and a handful of wheat flour. Melt a quarter of a pound of fresh butter in a quart of milk. Beat four eggs very light, and stir into them alternately (a little at a time of each) the milk when it is quite cold, and the meal; adding a small tea-spoonful of salt. The whole must be beaten long and hard. Then butter some muffin rings; set them on a hot griddle, and pour some of the batter into each.

Send the muffins to table hot, and split them by pulling them open with your fingers, as a knife will make them heavy. Eat them with butter, molasses or honey.

WATER MUFFINS.

Put four table-spoonfuls of fresh strong yeast into a pint of lukewarm water. Add a little salt; about a small tea-spoonful; then stir in gradually as much sifted flour as will make a thick batter. Cover the pan, and set it in a warm place to rise. When it is quite light, and your griddle is hot, grease and set your muffin rings on it; having first buttered them round the inside. Dip out a ladle full of the batter for each ring, and bake them over a quick fire. Send them to table hot, and split them by pulling open with your hands.

COMMON MUFFINS.

Having melted three table-spoonfuls of fresh butter in three pints of warm milk, set it away to cool. Then beat three eggs as light as possible, and stir them gradually into the milk when it is quite cold; adding a tea-spoonful of salt. Stir in by degrees enough of sifted flour to make a batter as thick as you can conveniently beat it; and lastly, add two table-spoonfuls of strong fresh yeast from the brewery. Cover the batter and set it in a warm place to rise. It should be light in about three hours. Having heated your griddle, grease it with some butter tied in a rag; grease your muffin rings round the inside, and set them on the griddle. Take some batter out of the pan with a ladle or a large spoon, pour it lightly into the rings, and bake the muffins of a light brown. When done, break or split them open with your fingers; butter them and send them to table hot.

SODA BISCUITS.

Melt half a pound of butter in a pint of warm milk, adding a tea-spoonful of soda; and stir in by degrees half a pound of sugar. Then sift into a pan two pounds of flour; make a hole in the middle; pour in the milk, &c., and mix it with the flour into a dough. Put it on your paste-board, and knead it long and hard till it becomes very light. Roll it out into a sheet half an inch thick. Cut it into little round cakes with the top of a wine glass, or with a tin cutter of that size; prick the tops; lay them on tins sprinkled with flour, or in shallow iron pans; and bake them of a light brown in a quick oven; they will be done in a few minutes. These biscuits keep very well.

A SALLY LUNN.

This cake is called after the inventress. Sift into a pan a pound and a half of flour. Make a hole in the middle, and put in two ounces of butter warmed in a pint of milk, a salt-spoonful of salt, three well-beaten eggs, and two table-spoonfuls of the best fresh yeast. Mix the flour well into the other ingredients, and put the whole into a square tin pan that has been greased with butter. Cover it, set it in a warm place, and when it is quite light, bake it in a moderate oven. Send it to table hot, and eat it with butter.

Or, you may bake it on a griddle, in small muffin rings, pulling the cakes open and buttering them when brought to table.

SHORT CAKES.

Rub three quarters of a pound of fresh butter into a pound and a half of sifted flour; and make it into a dough with a little cold water. Roll it out into a sheet half an inch thick, and cut it into round cakes with the edge of a tumbler. Prick them with a fork; lay them in a shallow iron pan sprinkled with flour, and bake them in a moderate oven till they are brown. Send them to table hot; split and butter them.

TEA BISCUIT.

Melt a quarter of a pound of fresh butter in a quart of warm milk, and add a salt-spoonful of salt. Sift two pounds of flour into a pan, make a hole in the centre, and put in three table-spoonfuls of the best brewer's yeast. Add the milk and butter and mix it into a stiff paste. Cover it and set it by the fire to rise. When quite light, knead it well, roll it out an inch thick, and cut it into round cakes with the edge of a tumbler. Prick the top of each with a fork; lay them in buttered pans and bake them light brown. Send them to table warm, and split and butter them.

RICE CAKES.

Pick and wash half a pint of rice, and boil it very soft. Then drain it, and let it get cold. Sift a pint and a half of flour over the pan of rice, and mix in a quarter of a pound of butter that has been warmed by the fire, and a salt-spoonful of salt. Beat five eggs very light, and stir them gradually into a quart of milk. Beat the whole very hard, and bake it in muffin rings, or in waffle-irons. Send them to table hot, and eat them with butter, honey, or molasses. You may make these cakes of rice flour instead of mixing together whole rice and wheat flour.

CREAM CAKES.

Having beaten three eggs very light, stir them into a quart of cream alternately with a quart of sifted flour; and add one wine glass of strong yeast, and a salt-spoon of salt. Cover the batter, and set it near the fire to rise. When it is quite light, stir in a large table-spoonful of butter that has been warmed by the fire. Bake the cakes in muffin rings, and send them to table hot, split with your fingers, and buttered.

FRENCH ROLLS.

Sift a pound of flour into a pan, and rub into it two ounces of butter; mix in the whites only of three eggs, beaten to a stiff froth, and a table-spoonful of strong yeast; add sufficient milk to make a stiff dough, and a salt-spoonful of salt. Cover it and set it before the fire to rise. It should be light in an hour. Then put it on a paste-board, divide it into rolls, or round cakes; lay them in a floured square pan, and bake them about ten minutes in a quick oven.

COMMON ROLLS.

Sift two pounds of flour into a pan, and mix with it a tea-spoonful of salt. Warm together a jill of water and a jill of milk. Make a hole in the middle of the pan of flour; mix with the milk and water a jill of the best yeast, and pour it into the hole. Mix into the liquid enough of the surrounding flour to make a thin batter, which you must stir till quite smooth and free from lumps. Then strew a handful of flour over the top, and set it in a warm, place to rise for two hours or more. When it is quite light, and has cracked on the top, make it into a dough with some more milk and water. Knead it well for ten minutes. Cover it, and set it again to rise for twenty minutes. Then make the dough into rolls or round balls. Bake them in a square pan, and send them to table hot, cut in three, buttered and put together again.

BREAD.

Take one peck or two gallons of fine wheat flour, and sift it into a kneading trough, or into a small clean tub, or a large broad earthen pan; and make a deep hole in the middle of the heap of flour, to begin the process by what is called setting a sponge. Have ready half a pint of warm water, which in summer should be only lukewarm, but even in winter it must not be hot or boiling, and stir it well into half a pint of strong fresh yeast; (if the yeast is home-made you must use from three quarters to a whole pint;) then pour it into the hole in the middle of the flour. With a spoon work in the flour round the edges of the liquid, so as to bring in by degrees sufficient flour to form a thin batter, which must be well stirred about, for a minute or two. Then take a handful of flour, and scatter it thinly over the top of this batter, so as to cover it entirely. Lay a warmed cloth over the whole, and set it to rise in a warm place; in winter put it nearer the fire than in summer. When the batter has risen so as to make cracks in the flour on the top, scatter over it three or four table-spoonfuls (not more) of fine salt, and begin to form the whole mass into a dough; commencing round the hole containing the batter, and pouring as much soft water as is necessary to make the flour mix with the batter; the water must never be more than lukewarm. When the whole is well mixed, and the original batter which is to give fermentation to the dough is completely incorporated with it, knead it hard, turning it over, pressing it, folding it, and working it thoroughly with your clenched hands for twenty minutes or half an hour; or till it becomes perfectly light and stiff. The goodness of bread depends much on the kneading, which to do well requires strength and practice. When it has been sufficiently worked, form the dough into a lump in the middle of the trough or pan, and scatter a little dry flour thinly over it; then cover it, and set it again in a warm place to undergo a farther fermentation; for which, if all has been done rightly, about twenty minutes or half an hour will be sufficient. The oven should be hot by the time the dough has remained twenty minutes in the lump. If it is a brick oven it should be heated by faggots or small light wood, allowed to remain in till burnt down into coals. When the bread is ready, clear out the coals, and sweep and wipe the floor of the oven clean. Introduce nothing wet into the oven, as it may crack the bricks when they are hot. Try the heat of the bottom by throwing in some flour; and if it scorches and burns black, do not venture to put in the bread till the oven has had time to become cooler. Put the dough on the paste-board, (which must be sprinkled with flour,) and divide it into loaves, forming them of a good shape. Place them in the oven, and close up the door, which you may open once or twice to see how the bread is going on. The loaves will bake in from two hours and a half to three hours, or more, according to their size. When the loaves are done, wrap each in a clean coarse towel, and stand them up on end to cool slowly. It is a good way to have the cloths previously made damp by sprinkling them plentifully with water, and letting them lie awhile rolled up tightly. This will make the crust of the bread less dry and hard. Bread should be kept always wrapped in a cloth, and covered from the air in a box or basket with a close lid. Unless you have other things to bake at the same time, it is not worth while to heat a brick oven for a small quantity of bread. Two or three loaves can be baked very well in a stove, (putting them into square iron pans,) or in a Dutch oven. [Footnote: If you bake bread in a Dutch oven, take off the lid when the loaf is done, and let it remain in the oven uncovered for a quarter of an hour.] If the bread has been mixed over night (which should never be done in warm weather) and is found, on tasting it, to be sour in the morning, melt a tea-spoonful of pearl-ash in a little milk-warm water, and sprinkle it over the dough; let it set half an hour, and then knead it. This will remove the acidity, and rather improve the bread in lightness. If dough is allowed to freeze it is totally spoiled. All bread that is sour, heavy, or ill-baked is not only unpalatable, but extremely unwholesome, and should never be eaten. These accidents so frequently happen when bread is made at home by careless, unpractised or incompetent persons, that families who live in cities or towns will generally risk less and save more, by obtaining their bread from a professional baker. If you like a little Indian in your wheat bread, prepare rather a larger quantity of warm water for setting the sponge; stirring into the water, while it is warming, enough of sifted Indian meal to make it like thin gruel. Warm water that has had pumpkin boiled in it is very good for bread. Strong fresh yeast from the brewery should always be used in preference to any other. If the yeast is home-made, or not very strong and fresh, double or treble the quantity mentioned in the receipt will be necessary to raise the bread. On the other hand, if too much yeast is put in, the bread will be disagreeably bitter. [Footnote: If you are obliged from its want of strength to put in a large quantity of yeast, mix with it two or three handfuls of bran; add the warm water to it, and then strain it through a sieve or cloth; or you may correct the bitterness by putting in a few bits of charcoal and then straining it.] You may take off a portion of the dough that has been prepared for bread, make it up into little round cakes or rolls, and bake them for breakfast or tea.

BRAN BREAD.

Sift into a pan three quarts of unbolted wheat meal. Stir a jill of strong yeast, and a jill of molasses into a quart of soft water, (which must be warm but not hot,) and add a small tea-spoonful of pearl-ash, or sal-aratus. Make a hole in the heap of flour, pour in the liquid, and proceed in the usual manner of making bread. This quantity may be made into two loaves. Bran bread is considered very wholesome; and is recommended to persons afflicted with dyspepsia.

RYE AND INDIAN BREAD.

Sift two quarts of rye, and two quarts of Indian meal, and mix them well together. Boil three pints of milk; pour it boiling hot upon the meal; add two tea-spoonfuls of salt, and stir the whole very hard. Let it stand till it becomes of only a lukewarm heat, and then stir in half a pint of good fresh yeast; if from the brewery and quite fresh, a smaller quantity will suffice. Knead the mixture into a stiff dough, and set it to rise in a pan. Cover it with a thick cloth that has been previously warmed, and set it near the fire. When it is quite light, and has cracked all over the top, make it into two loaves, put them into a moderate oven, and bake them two hours and a half.

COMMON YEAST.

Put a large handful of hops into two quarts of boiling water, which must then be set on the fire again, and boiled twenty minutes with the hops. Have ready in a pan three pints of sifted flour; strain the liquid, and pour half of it on the flour. Let the other half stand till it becomes cool, and then mix it gradually into the pan with the flour, &c. Then stir into it half a pint of good strong yeast, fresh from the brewery if possible; if not, use some that was left of the last making. You may increase the strength by stirring into your yeast before you bottle it, four or five large tea-spoonfuls of brown sugar, or as many table-spoonfuls of molasses.

Put it into clean bottles, and cork them loosely till the fermentation is over. Next morning put in the corks tightly, and set the bottles in a cold place. When you are going to bottle the yeast it will be an improvement to place two or three raisins at the bottom of each bottle. It is best to make yeast very frequently; as, with every precaution, it will scarcely keep good a week, even in cold weather. If you are apprehensive of its becoming sour, put into each bottle a lump of pearl-ash the size of a hazle-nut.

BRAN YEAST.

Mix a pint of wheat bran, and a handful of hops with a quart of water, and boil them together about twenty minutes. Then strain it through a sieve into a pan; when the liquid becomes only milk-warm, stir into it four table-spoonfuls of brewer's yeast, and two of brown sugar, or four of molasses.

Put it into a wooden bowl, cover it, and set it near the fire for four or five hours. Then bottle it, and cork it tightly next day.

PUMPKIN YEAST.

Pare a fine ripe pumpkin, and cut it into pieces. Put them into a kettle with a large handful of hops, and as much water as will cover them. Boil them till the pumpkin is soft enough to pass through a cullender. Having done this, put the pulp into a stone jar, adding half a pint of good strong yeast to set it into a fermentation. The yeast must be well stirred into the pumpkin. Leave the jar uncovered till next day; then secure it lightly with a cork. If pumpkin yeast is well made, and of a proper consistence, neither too thick nor too thin, it will keep longer than any other.

BAKER'S YEAST.

To a gallon of soft water put two quarts of wheat bran, one quart of ground malt, (which may be obtained from a brewery,) and two handfuls of hops. Boil them together for half an hour. Then strain it through a sieve, and let it stand till it is cold; after which put to it two large tea-cups of molasses, and half a pint of strong yeast. Pour it into a stone jug, and let it stand uncorked till next morning. Then pour off the thin liquid from the top, and cork the jug tightly. When you are going to use the yeast, if it has been made two or three days, stir in a little pearl-ash dissolved in warm water, allowing a lump the size of a hickory-nut to a pint of yeast. This will correct any tendency to sourness, and make the yeast more brisk.

TO MAKE BUTTER.

Scald your milk pans every day after washing them; and let them set till the water gets cold. Then wipe them with a clean cloth. Fill them all with cold water half an hour before milking time, and do not pour it out till the moment before you are ready to use the pans. Unless all the utensils are kept perfectly sweet and nice, the cream and butter will never be good. Empty milk-pans should stand all day in the sun.

When you have strained the milk into the pans, (which should be broad and shallow,) place them in the spring-house, setting them down in the water. After the milk has stood twenty-four hours, skim off the cream, and deposits it in a large deep earthen jar, commonly called a crock, which must be kept closely covered, and stirred up with a stick at least twice a day, and whenever you add fresh cream to it. This stirring is to prevent the butter from being injured by the skin that will gather over the top of the cream.

You should churn at least twice a week, for if the cream is allowed to stand too long, the butter will inevitably have a odd taste. Add to the cream the strippings of the milk. Butter of only two or three days gathering is the best. With four or five good cows, you may easily manage to have a churning every three days. If your dairy is on a large scale, churn every two days.

Have your churn very clean, and rinse and cool it with cold water. A barrel churn is best; though a small upright one, worked by a staff or dash, will do very well where there are but one or two cows.

Strain the cream from the crock into the churn, and put on the lid. Move the handle slowly in warm weather, as churning too fast will make the butter soft. When you find that the handle moves heavily and with great difficulty, the butter has come; that is, it has separated from the thin fluid and gathered into a lump, and it then is not necessary to churn any longer. Take it out with a wooden ladle, and put it into a small tub or pail. Squeeze and press it hard with the ladle, to get out all that remains of the milk. Add a little salt, and then squeeze and work It for a long time. If any of the milk is allowed to remain in, it will speedily turn sour and spoil the butter. Set it away in a cool place for three hours, and then work it over again. [Footnote: A marble slab or table will be found of great advantage in working and making up butter.] Wash it in cold water; weigh it; make it up into separate pounds, smoothing, and shaping it; and clap each pound on your wooden butter print, dipping the print every time in cold water. Spread a clean linen cloth on a bench in the spring-house; place the butter on it, and let it set till it becomes perfectly hard. Then wrap each pound in a separate piece of linen that has been dipped in cold water.

Pour the buttermilk into a clean crock, and place it in the spring-house, with a saucer to dip it out with. Keep the pot covered. The buttermilk will be excellent the first day; but afterwards it will become too thick and sour. Winter buttermilk is never very palatable.

Before you put away the churn, wash and scald it well; and the day that you use it again, keep it for an hour or more filled with cold water.

In cold weather, churning is a much more tedious process than in summer, as the butter will be longer coming. It is best then to have the churn in a warm room, or near the fire. If you wish to prepare the butter for keeping a long time, take it after it has been thoroughly well made, and pack it down tightly into a large jar. You need not in working it, add more salt than if the butter was to be eaten immediately. But preserve it by making a brine of fine salt, dissolved in water. The brine must be strong enough to bear up an egg on the surface without sinking. Strain the brine into the jar, so as to be about two inches above the butter. Keep the jar closely covered, and set it in a cool place.

When you want any of the butter for use, take it off evenly from the top; so that the brine may continue to cover it at a regular depth.

This receipt for making butter is according to the method in use at the best farm-houses in Pennsylvania, and if exactly followed will be found very good. The badness of butter is generally owing to carelessness or mismanagement; to keeping the cream too long without churning; to want of cleanliness in the utensils; to not taking the trouble to work it sufficiently; or to the practice of salting it so profusely as to render it unpleasant to the taste, and unfit for cakes or pastry. All these causes of bad butter are inexcusable, and can easily be avoided. Unless the cows have been allowed to feed where there are bitter weeds or garlic, the milk cannot naturally have any disagreeable taste, and therefore the fault of the butter must be the fault of the maker. Of course, the cream is much richer where the pasture is fine and luxuriant; and in winter, when the cows have only dry food, the butter must be consequently whiter and more insipid than in the grazing season. Still, if properly made, even winter butter cannot taste badly.

Many economical housekeepers always buy for cooking, butter of inferior quality. This is a foolish practice; as when it is bad, the taste will predominate through all attempts to disguise it, and render every thing unpalatable with which it is combined. As the use of butter is designed to improve and not to spoil the flavour of cookery, it is better to omit it altogether, and to substitute something else, unless you can procure that which is good. Lard, suet, beef-drippings, and sweet oil, may be used in the preparation of various dishes; and to eat with bread or warm cakes, honey, molasses, or stewed fruit, &c, are far superior to bad butter.

CHEESE.

In making good cheese, skim milk is never used. The milk should either be warm from the cow or heated to that temperature over the fire. When the rennet is put in, the heat of the milk should be from 90 to 96 degrees. Three quarts of milk will yield, on an average, about a pound of cheese. In infusing the rennet, allow a quart of lukewarm water, and a table-spoonful of salt to a piece about half the size of your hand. The rennet must soak all night in the water before it can be fit for use. In the morning (after taking as much of it as you want) put the rennet water into a bottle and cork it tightly. It will keep the better for adding to it a wine glass of brandy. If too large a proportion of rennet is mixed with the milk, the cheese will be tough and leathery.

To make a very good cheese, take three buckets of milk warm from the cow, and strain it immediately into a large tub or kettle. Stir into it half a tea-cupful of infusion of rennet or rennet-water; and having covered it, set it in a warm place for about half an hour, or till it becomes a firm curd. Cut the curd into squares with a large knife, or rather with a wooden slitting-dish, and let it stand about fifteen minutes. Then break it up fine with your hands, and let it stand a quarter of an hour longer. Then pour off from the top as much of the whey as you can; tie up the curd in a linen cloth or bag, and hang it up to drain out the remainder of the whey; setting a pan under it to catch the droppings. After all the whey is drained out, put the curd into the cheese-tray, and cut it again into slices; chop it coarse; put a cloth about it; place it in the cheese-hoop or mould, and set it in the screw press for half an hour, pressing it hard. [Footnote: If you are making cheese on a small scale, and have not a regular press, put the curd (after you have wrapped it in a cloth) into a small circular wooden box or tub with numerous holes bored in the bottom; and with a lid that fits the inside exactly. Lay heavy weights on the lid in such a manner as to press evenly all over.] Then take it out; chop the curd very fine; add salt to your taste; and put it again into the cheese-hoop with a cloth about it, and press it again. You must always wet the cloth all over to prevent its sticking to the cheese, and tearing the surface. Let it remain in the press till next morning, when you must take it out and turn it; then wrap it in a clean wet cloth, and replace it in the press, where it must remain all day. On the following morning again take out the cheese; turn it, renew the cloth, and put it again into the press. Three days pressing will be sufficient.

When you finally take it out of the press, grease the cheese all over with lard, and put it on a clean shelf in a dry dark room, or in a wire safe. Wipe, grease, and turn it carefully every day. If you omit this a single day the cheese will spoil. Keep the shelf perfectly clean, and see that the cheese does not stick to it. When the cheese becomes firm, you may omit the greasing; but continue to rub it all over every day with a clean dry cloth. Continue this for five or sis weeks; the cheese will then be fit to eat.

The best time for making cheese is when the pasture is in perfection.

You may enrich the colour of the cheese by a little anatto or arnotta; of which procure a small quantity from the druggist, powder it, tie it in a muslin rag, and hold it in the warm milk, (after it is strained,) pressing out the colouring matter with your fingers, as laundresses press their indigo or blue rag in the tub of water. Anatto is perfectly harmless.

After they begin to dry, (or ripen, as it is called,) it is the custom in some dairy-farms, to place the cheeses in the haystack, and keep them there among the hay for five or six weeks. This is said greatly to improve their consistence and flavour. Cheeses are sometimes ripened by putting them every day in fresh grass.

SAGE CHEESE.

Take some of the young top leaves of the sage plant, and pound them in a mortar till you have extracted the juice. Put the juice into a bowl, wipe cut the mortar, put in some spinach leaves, and pound them till you have an equal quantity of spinach juice. Mix the two juices together, and stir them into the warm milk immediately after you have put in the rennet. You may use sage juice alone; but the spinach will greatly improve the colour; besides correcting the bitterness of the sage.

STILTON CHEESE.

Having strained the morning's milk, and skimmed the cream from the milk of the preceding evening, mix the cream and the new milk together while the latter is quite warm, and stir in the rennet-water. When the curd has formed, you must not break it up, (as is done with other cheese,) but take it out all at once with a wooden skimming dish, and place it on a sieve to drain gradually. While it is draining, keep pressing it gently till it becomes firm and dry. Then lay a clean cloth at the bottom of a wooden cheese-hoop or mould, which should have a few small holes bored in the bottom. The cloth must be large enough for the end to turn over the top again, after the curd is put in. Place it in the press for two hours; turn it, (putting a clean cloth under it,) and press it again for six or eight hours. Then turn it again, rub the cheese all over with salt, and return it to the press for fourteen hours. Should the edges of the cheese project, they must be pared off.

When you take it finally out of the press, bind it round tightly with a cloth, (which must be changed every day when you turn the cheese,) and set it on a shelf or board. Continue the cloths till the cheese is firm enough to support itself; rubbing or brushing the outside every day when you turn it. After the cloths are left off, continue to brush the cheese every day for two or three months; during which time it may be improved by keeping it covered all round, under and over, with grass, which must be renewed every day, and gathered when quite dry after the dew is off. Keep the cheese and the grass between two large plates.

A Stilton cheese is generally made of a small size, seldom larger in circumference than a dinner plate, and about four or five inches thick. They are usually put up for keeping, in cases of sheet lead, fitting them exactly. There is no cheese superior to them in richness and mildness.

Cream cheeses (as they are generally called) may be made in this manner. They are always eaten quite fresh, while the inside is still somewhat soft. They are made small, and are sent to table whole, cut across into triangular slices like a pie or cake. After they become fit to eat, they will keep good but a day or two, but they are considered while fresh very delicious.

COTTAGE CHEESE.

This is that preparation of milk vulgarly called Smear Case. Take a pan of milk that has just began to turn sour; cover it, and set it by the fire till it becomes a curd. Pour off the whey from the top, and tie up the curd in a pointed linen bag, and hang it up to drain; setting something under it to catch the droppings. Do not squeeze it. Let it drain all night, and in the morning put the curd into a pan, (adding some rich cream,) and work it very fine with a spoon, chopping and pressing it till about the consistency of a soft bread pudding. To a soup plate of the fine curd put a tea-spoonful of salt; and a piece of butter about the size of a walnut; mixing all thoroughly together. Having prepared the whole in this manner, put it into a stone or china vessel; cover it closely, and set it in a cold place till tea time. You may make it of milk that is entirely sweet by forming the curd with rennet.

A WELSH RABBIT.

Toast some slices of bread, (having cut off the crust,) butter them, and keep them hot. Grate or shave down with a knife some fine mellow cheese: and, if it is not very rich, mix with it a few small bits of butter. Put it into a cheese-toaster, or into a skillet, and add to it a tea-spoonful of made mustard; a little cayenne pepper; and if you choose, a wine glass of fresh porter or of red wine. Stir the mixture over hot coals, till it is completely dissolved; and then brown it by holding over it a salamander, or a red-hot shovel. Lay the toast in the bottom and round the sides of a deep dish; put the melted cheese upon it, and serve it up as hot as possible, with dry toast in a separate plate; and accompanied by porter or ale.

This preparation of cheese is for a plain supper.

Dry cheese is frequently grated on little plates for the tea-table.

TO MAKE CHOCOLATE

To each square of a chocolate cake allow three jills, or a chocolate cup and a half of boiling water. Scrape down the chocolate with a knife, and mix it first to a paste with a small quantity of the hot water; just enough to melt it in. Then put it into a block tin pot with the remainder of the water; set it on hot coals; cover it, and let it boil (stirring it twice) till the liquid is one third reduced. Supply that third with cream or rich milk; stir it again, and take it off the fire. Serve it up as hot as possible, with dry toast, or dry rusk. It chills immediately. If you wish it frothed, pour it into the cup, and twirl round in it the little wooden instrument called a chocolate mill, till you nave covered the top with foam.

TO MAKE TEA.

In buying tea, it is best to get it by the box, of an importer, that you may be sure of having it fresh, and unmixed with any that is old and of inferior quality. The box should be kept in a very dry place. If green tea is good, it will look green in the cup when poured out. Black tea should be dark coloured and have a fragrant flowery smell. The best pots for making tea are those of china. Metal and Wedgwood tea-pots by frequent use will often communicate a disagreeable taste to the tea. This disadvantage may be remedied in Wedgwood ware, by occasionally boiling the tea-pots in a vessel of hot water.

In preparing to make tea, let the pot be twice scalded from the tea-kettle, which must be boiling hard at the moment the water is poured on the tea; otherwise it will be weak and insipid, even when a large quantity is put in. The best way is to have a chafing dish, with a kettle always boiling on it, in the room where the tea is made. It is a good rule to allow two tea-spoonfuls of tea to half a pint or a large cupful of water, or two tea-spoonfuls for each grown person that is to drink tea, and one spoonful extra. The pot being twice scalded, put in the tea, and pour on the water about ten minutes before you want to fill the cups, that it may have time to draw or infuse. Have hot water in another pot, to weaken the cups of those that like it so. That the second course of cups may be as strong as the first, put some tea into a cup just before you sit down to table, pour on it a very little boiling water, (just enough to cover it,) set a saucer over it to keep in the steam, and let it infuse till you have filled all the first cups; then add it to that already in the tea-pot, and pour in a little boiling water from the kettle. Except that it is less convenient for a large family, a kettle on a chafing dish is better than an urn, as the water may be kept longer boiling.

In making black tea, use a larger quantity than of green, as it is of a much weaker nature. The best black teas in general use are pekoe and pouchong; the best green teas are imperial, young hyson, and gunpowder.

TO MAKE COFFEE.

The manner in which coffee is roasted is of great importance to its flavour. If roasted too little, it will be weak and insipid; if too much, the taste will be bitter and unpleasant. To have it very good, it should be roasted immediately before it is made, doing no more than the quantity you want at that time. It loses much of its strength by keeping, even in twenty-four hours after roasting. It should on no consideration be ground till directly before it is made. Every family should be provided with a coffee roaster, which is an iron cylinder to stand before the fire, and is either turned by a handle, or wound up like a jack to go of itself. If roasted in an open pot or pan, much of the flavour evaporates in the process. Before the coffee is put into the roaster, it should be carefully examined and picked, lest there should be stones or bad grains among it. It should be roasted of a bright brown; and will be improved by putting among it a piece of butter when about half done.

Watch it carefully while roasting, looking at it frequently.

A coffee-mill affixed to the wall is far more convenient than one that must he held on the lap. It is best to grind the coffee while warm.

Allow half a pint of ground coffee to three pints of water. If the coffee is not freshly roasted, you should put in more. Put the water into the tin coffee-pot, and set it on hot coals; when it boils, put in the coffee, a spoonful at a time, (stirring it between each spoonful,) and add two or three chips of isinglass, or the white of an egg. Stir it frequently, till it has risen up to the top in boiling; then set it a little farther from the fire, and boil it gently for ten minutes, or a quarter of an hour; after which pour in a tea-cup of cold water, and put it in the corner to settle for ten minutes. Scald your silver or china pot, and transfer the coffee to it; carefully pouring it off from the grounds, so as not to disturb them.

If coffee is allowed to boil too long, it will lose much of its strength, and also become sour.

FRENCH COFFEE.

To make coffee without boiling, you must have a biggin, the best sort of which is what in France is called a Grecque. They are to be had of various sizes and prices at the tin stores. Coffee made in this manner is much less troublesome than when boiled, and requires no white of egg or isinglass to clear it. The coffee should be freshly roasted and ground. Allow two cupfuls of ground coffee to sis cupfuls of boiling water. Having first scalded the biggin, (which should have strainers of perforated tin, and not of linen,) put in the coffee, and pour on the water, which should be boiling hard at the time. Shut down the lid, place the pot near the fire, and the coffee will be ready as soon as it has all drained through the coarse and fine strainers into the receiver below the spout. Scald your china or silver pot, and pour the coffee into it. But it is best to have a biggin in the form of an urn, in which the coffee can both be made and brought to table.

For what is called milk coffee,—boil the milk or cream separately; bring it to table in a covered vessel, and pour it hot into the coffee, the flavour of which will be impaired if the milk is boiled with it.

DOMESTIC LIQUORS ETC.

SPRUCE BEER

Put into a large kettle, ten gallons of water, a quarter of a pound of hops, and a tea-cupful of ginger. Boil them together till all the hops sink to the bottom. Then dip out a bucket full of the liquor, and stir into it six quarts of molasses, and three ounces and a half of the essence of spruce. When all is dissolved, mix it with the liquor in the kettle; strain it through a hair sieve into a cask; and stir well into it half a pint of good strong yeast. Let it ferment a day or two; then bung up the cask, and you may bottle the beer the next day. It will be fit for use in a week.

For the essence of spruce, you may substitute two pounds of the outer sprigs of the spruce fir, boiled ten minutes in the liquor.

To make spruce beer for present use, and in a smaller quantity, boil a handful of hops in two gallons and a half of water, till they fall to the bottom, Then strain the water, and when it is lukewarm, stir into it a table-spoonful of ground white ginger; a pint of molasses; a table-spoonful of essence of spruce; and half a pint of yeast. Mix the whole well together in a stone jug, and let it ferment for a day and a half, or two days. Then put it into bottles, with three or four raisins in the bottom of each, to prevent any further fermentation. It will then be fit for immediate use.

GINGER BEER.

Break up a pound and a half of loaf-sugar, and mix with it three ounces of strong white ginger, and the grated peel of two lemons. Put these ingredients into a large stone jar, and pour over them two gallons of boiling water. When it becomes milk-warm strain it, and add the juice of the lemons and two large table-spoonfuls of strong yeast. Make this beer in the evening and let it stand all night. Next morning bottle it in little half pint stone bottles, tying down the corks with twine.

MOLASSES BEER.

To six quarts of water, add two quarts of West India molasses; half a pint of the best brewer's yeast; two table-spoonfuls of ground ginger; and one table-spoonful of cream of tartar. Stir all together. Let it stand twelve hours, and then bottle it, putting three or four raisins into each bottle.

It will be much improved by substituting the juice and grated peel of a large lemon, for one of the spoonfuls of ginger.

Molasses beer keeps good but two or three days.

SASSAFRAS BEER.

Have ready two gallons of soft water; one quart of wheat bran; a large handful of dried apples; half a pint of molasses; a small handful of hops; half a pint of strong fresh yeast, and a piece of sassafras root the size of an egg.

Put all the ingredients (except the molasses and yeast) at once into a large kettle. Boil it till the apples are quite soft. Put the molasses into a small clean tub or a large pan. Set a hair sieve over the vessel, and strain the mixture through it. Let it stand till it becomes only milk-warm, and then stir in the yeast. Put the liquor immediately into the keg or jugs, and let it stand uncorked to ferment. Fill the jugs quite full, that the liquor in fermenting may run over. Set them in a large tub. When you see that the fermentation or working has subsided, cork it, and it will be fit for use next day.

Two large table-spoonfuls of ginger stirred into the molasses will be found an improvement.

If the yeast is stirred in while the liquor is too warm, it will be likely to turn sour.

If the liquor is not put immediately into the jugs, it will not ferment well.

Keep it in a cold place. It will not in warm weather be good more than two days. It is only made for present use.

GOOSEBERRY WINE.

Allow three gallons of soft water (measured after it has boiled an hour) to six gallons of gooseberries, which must be full ripe. Top and tail the gooseberries; put them, a few at a time, into a wooden dish, and with a rolling-pin or beetle break and mash every one; transferring them, as they are done, into a large stone jar. Pour the boiling water upon the mashed gooseberries; cover the jar, and let them stand twelve hours. Then strain and measure the juice, and to each quart allow three-quarters of a pound of loaf-sugar; mix it with the liquid, and let it stand eight or nine hours to dissolve, stirring it several times.

Then pour it into a keg of proper size for containing it, and let it ferment at the bung-hole; filling it up as it works out with some of the liquor reserved for that purpose. As soon as it ceases to hiss, stop it close with a cloth wrapped round the bung. A pint of white brandy for every gallon of the gooseberry wine may be added on bunging it up. At the end of four or five months it will probably be fine enough to bottle off. It is best to bottle it in cold frosty weather. You may refine it by allowing to every gallon of wine the whites of two eggs, beaten to a froth, with a very small tea-spoonful of salt. When the white of egg, &c, is a stiff froth, take out a quart of the wine, and mix them well together. Then pour it into the cask, and in a few days it will be fine and clear. You may begin to use it any time after it is bottled. Put two or three raisins in the bottom of each bottle. They will tend to keep the wine from any farther fermentation.

Fine gooseberry wine has frequently passed for champagne. Keep the bottles in saw-dust, lying on their sides.

CURRANT WINE.

Take four gallons of ripe currants; strip them from the stalks into a great stone jar that has a cover to it, and mash them with a long thick stick. Let them stand twenty-four hours; then put the currants into a large linen bag; wash out the jar, set it under the bag, and squeeze the juice into it. Boil together two gallons and a half of water, and five pounds and a half of the best loaf-sugar, skimming it well. When the scum ceases to rise, mix the syrup with the currant juice. Let it stand a fortnight or three weeks to settle; and then transfer it to another vessel, taking care not to disturb the lees or dregs. If it is not quite clear and bright, refine it by mixing with a quart of the wine, (taken out for the purpose,) the whites of two eggs beaten to a stiff froth, and half an ounce of cream of tartar. Pour this gradually into the vessel. Let it stand ten days, and then bottle it off. Place the bottles in saw-dust, laying them on their sides. Take care that the saw-dust is not from pine wood. The wine will be fit to drink in a year, but is better when three or four years old.

You may add a little brandy to it when you make it; allowing a quart of brandy to six gallons of wine.

RASPBERRY WINE.

Put four gallons of ripe raspberries into a stone jar, and mash them with a round stick. Take four gallons of soft water, (measured after it has boiled an hour,) and strain it warm over the raspberries. Stir it well and let it stand twelve hours. Then strain it through a bag, and to every gallon of liquor put three pounds of loaf-sugar. Set it over a clear fire, and boil and skim it till the scum ceases to rise. When it is cold bottle it. Open the bottles every day for a fortnight, closing them again in a few minutes. Then seal the corks, and lay the bottles on their sides in saw-dust, which must not be from pine wood.

ELDERBERRY WINE.

Gather the elderberries when quite ripe; put them into a stone jar, mash them with a round stick, and set them in a warm oven, or in a large kettle of boiling water till the jar is hot through, and the berries begin to simmer. Then take them out, and press and strain them through a sieve. To every quart of juice allow a pound of Havanna or Lisbon sugar, and two quarts of cold soft water. Put the sugar into a large kettle, pour the juice over it, and, when it has dissolved, stir in the water. Set the kettle over the fire, an& boil and skim it till the scum ceases to rise. To four gallons of the liquor add a pint and a half of brandy. Put it into a keg, and let it stand with the bung put in loosely for four or five days, by which time it will have ceased to ferment. Then stop it closely, plastering the bung with clay. At the end of six months, draw off a little of it; and if it is not quite clear and bright, refine it with the whites and shells of three or four eggs, beaten to a stiff froth and stirred into a quart of the wine, taken out for the purpose and then returned to the cask; or you may refine it with an ounce or more of dissolved isinglass. Let it stand a week or two, and then bottle it.

This is an excellent domestic wine, very common in England, and deserving to be better known in America, where the elderberry tree is found in great abundance. Elderberry wine is generally taken mulled with spice, and warm.

ELDER FLOWER WINE.

Take the flowers or blossoms of the elder tree, and strip them from the stalks. To every quart of flowers allow one gallon of water, and three pounds of while sugar. Boil and skim the sugar and water, and then pour it hot on the flowers. When cool, mix in with it some lemon juice and some yeast; allowing to six gallons of the liquor the juice of six lemons, and four or five table-spoonfuls of good yeast stirred in very hard. Let it ferment for three days in a tub covered with a double blanket. Then strain the wine through a sieve, (add six whites of eggs beaten to a stiff froth, or an ounce of melted isinglass,) and put it into a cask, in the bottom of which you have laid four or five pounds of the best raisins, stoned. Stop the cask closely, and in six months the wine will be fit to bottle. It will much resemble Frontiniac, the elder flowers imparting to it a very pleasant taste.

CIDER WINE.

Take sweet cider immediately from the press. Strain it through a flannel bag into a tub, and stir into it as much honey as will make it strong enough to bear up an egg. Then boil and skim it, and when the scum ceases to rise, strain it again. When cool, put it into a cask, and set it in a cool cellar till spring. Then bottle it off; and when ripe, it will be found a very pleasant beverage. The cider must be of the very best quality, made entirely from good sound apples.

MEAD.

To every gallon of water put five pounds of strained honey, (the water must be hot when you add the honey,) and boil it three quarters of an hour, skimming it well. Then put in some hops tied in a thin bag, (allowing an ounce or a handful to each gallon,) and let it boil half an hour longer. Strain it into a tub, and let it stand four days. Then put it into a cask, (or into a demijohn if the quantity is small,) adding for each gallon of mead a jill of brandy and a sliced lemon. If a large cask, do not bottle it till it has stood a year.

FOX GRAPE SHRUB.

Gather the grapes when they are full grown, but before they begin to purple. Pick from the stems a sufficient quantity to nearly fill a large preserving kettle, and pour on them as much boiling water as the kettle will hold. Set it over a brisk fire, and keep it scalding hot till all the grapes have burst. Then take them off, press out and strain the liquor, and allow to each quart a pound of sugar stirred well in. Dissolve the sugar in the juice; then put them together into a clean kettle, and boil and skim them for ten minutes, or till the scum ceases to rise. When cold, bottle it; first putting into each bottle a jill of brandy. Seal the bottles, and keep them in a warm closet.

You may make gooseberry shrub in this manner.

CURRANT SHRUB.

Your currants must be quite ripe. Pick them from the stalks, and squeeze them through a linen bag. To each quart of juice allow a pound of loaf-sugar. Put the sugar and juice into a preserving kettle, and let it melt before it goes on the fire. Boil it ten minutes, skimming it well. When cold, add a jill of the best white brandy to each quart of the juice. Bottle it, and set it away for use; sealing the corks. It improves by keeping.

Raspberry shrub may be made in this manner; also strawberry.

CHERRY SHRUB.

Pick from the stalks, and stone a sufficient quantity of ripe morellas, or other red cherries of the best and most juicy description. Put them with all their juice into a stone jar, and set it, closely covered, into a deep kettle of boiling water. Keep it boiling hard for a quarter of an hour. Then pour the cherries into a bag, and strain and press out all the juice. Allow a pound of sugar to a quart of juice, boil them together ten minutes in a preserving kettle, skimming them well, and when cold, bottle the liquid; first putting a jill of brandy into each bottle.

CHERRY BOUNCE.

Mix together six pounds of ripe morellas and six pounds of large black heart cherries. Put them into a wooden bowl or tub, and with a pestle or mallet mash them so as to crack all the stones. Mix with the cherries three pounds of loaf-sugar, or of sugar candy broken up, and put them into a demijohn, or into a large stone jar. Pour on two gallons of the best double rectified whiskey. Stop the vessel closely, and let it stand three months, shaking it every day during the first month. At the end of the three months you may strain the liquor and bottle it off. It improves by age.

LEMON SYRUP.

Break up into large pieces six pounds of fine loaf-sugar. Take twelve large ripe lemons, and (without cutting them) grate the yellow rind upon the sugar. Then, put the sugar, with the lemon gratings and two quarts of water, into a preserving kettle, and let it dissolve. When it is all melted, boil it till quite thick, skimming it till no more scum rises; it will then be done. Have ready the juice of all the lemons, and when the syrup is quite cold, stir in the lemon juice. Bottle it, and keep it in a cool place.

It makes a delicious drink in summer, in the proportion of one third lemon syrup and two thirds ice water.

LEMON CORDIAL.

Pare off very thin the yellow rind of a dozen large lemons; throw the parings into a gallon of white brandy, and let them steep till next day, or at least twelve hours. Break up four pounds of loaf-sugar into another vessel, and squeeze upon it the juice of the lemons. Let this too stand all night. Next day mix all together, boil two quarts of milk, and pour it boiling hot into the other ingredients. Cover the vessel, and let it stand eight days, stirring it daily. Then strain it through a flannel bag till the liquid is perfectly clear. Let it stand six weeks in a demijohn or glass jar, and then bottle it.

To make it still more clear, you may filter it through a piece of fine muslin pinned down to the bottom of a sieve, or through blotting paper, which must be frequently renewed. It should be white blotting paper.

ROSE CORDIAL.

Put a pound of fresh rose leaves into a tureen, with a quart of lukewarm water. Cover the vessel, and let them infuse for twenty-four hours. Then squeeze them through a linen bag till all the liquid is pressed out. Put a fresh pound of rose leaves into the tureen, pour the liquid back into it, and let it infuse again for two days. You may repeat this till you obtain a very strong infusion. Then to a pint of the infusion add half a pound of loaf-sugar, half a pint of white brandy, an ounce of broken cinnamon, and an ounce of coriander seeds. Put it into a glass jar, cover it well, and let it stand for two weeks. Then filter it through a fine muslin or a blotting paper (which must be white) pinned on the bottom of a sieve; and bottle it for use.

STRAWBERRY CORDIAL.

Hull a sufficient quantity of ripe strawberries, and squeeze them through a linen bag. To each quart of the juice allow a pint of white brandy, and half a pound of powdered loaf-sugar. Put the liquid into a glass jar or a demijohn, and let it stand a fortnight. Then filter it through a sieve, to the bottom of which a piece of fine muslin or blotting paper has been fastened; and afterwards bottle it,

RASPBERRY CORDIAL.

May be made in the above manner.

QUINCE CORDIAL.

Take the finest and ripest quinces you can procure, wipe them clean, and cut out all the defective parts. Then grate them into a tureen or some other large vessel, leaving out the seeds and cores. Let the grated pulp remain covered in the tureen for twenty-four hours. Then, squeeze it through a jelly-bag or cloth. To six quarts of the juice allow a quart of cold water, three pounds of loaf-sugar, (broken up,) and a quart of white brandy. Mix the whole well together, and put it into a stone jar. Have ready three very small flannel or thick muslin bags, (not larger than two inches square,) fill one with grated nutmeg, another with powdered mace, and the third with powdered cloves; and pat them, into the jar that the spice may flavour the liquor without mixing with it. Leave the jar uncorked for a few days; reserving some of the liquor to replace that which may flow over in the fermentation. Whenever it has done working, bottle it off, but do not use it for six months. If not sufficiently bright and clear, filter it through fine muslin, pinned round the bottom of a sieve, or through a white blotting paper fastened in the same manner.

PEACH CORDIAL.

Take the ripest and most juicy free-stone peaches you can procure. Cut them from the stones, and quarter them without paring. Crack the stones, and extract the kernels, which must be blanched and slightly pounded. Put the peaches into a large stone jar in layers, alternately with layers of the kernels, and of powdered loaf-sugar. When the jar is three parts full of the peaches, kernels, and sugar, fill it up with white brandy. Set the Jar in a large pan, and leave it uncovered for three or four days, in case of its fermenting and flowing over at the top. Fill up what is thus wasted with more brandy, and then close the jar tightly. Let it stand, five or six months; then filter it, and bottle it for use.

Cherry, apricot, and plum cordial may be made in the above manner; adding always the kernels.

ANNISEED CORDIAL.

Melt a pound of loaf-sugar in two quarts of water. Mix it with two quarts of white brandy, and add a table-spoonful of oil of anniseed. Let it stand a week; then filter it through, white blotting paper, and bottle it for use.

Clove or Cinnamon Corcial may be made in the same manner, by mixing sugar, water and brandy, and adding oil of cinnamon or oil of cloves. You may colour any of these cordials red by stirring in a little powdered cochineal that has been dissolved in a small quantity of brandy.

ROSE BRANDY.

Nearly fill a china or glass jar with freshly-gathered rose leaves, and pour in sufficient French white brandy to fill it quite up; and then cover it closely. Next day put the whole into a strainer, and having squeezed and pressed the rose leaves and drained off the liquid, throw away the leaves, put fresh ones into the jar, and return the brandy to it. Repeat this every day while roses are in season, (taking care to keep the jar well covered,) and you will find the liquid much better than rose water for flavouring cakes and puddings.

LEMON BRANDY.

When you use lemons for punch or lemonade, do not throw away the peels, but cut them in small pieces, and put them into a glass jar or bottle of brandy. You will find this brandy useful for many purposes.

In the same way keep for use the kernels of peach and plum stones, pounding them slightly before you put them into the brandy.

NOYAU.

Blanch and break up a pound of shelled bitter almonds or peach kernels. Mix with them the grated rinds of three large lemons, half a pint of clarified honey that has been boiled and skimmed, and three pounds of the best double-refined loaf-sugar. Put these ingredients into a jar or demijohn; pour in four quarts of the best white brandy or proof spirit; stop the vessel, and let it stand three months, shaking it every day for the first month. Then filter it, dilute it with rose water to your taste, (you may allow a quart of rose water to each quart of the liquor,) and bottle it for use.

This and any other cordial may be coloured red by mixing with it (after it is filtered) cochineal, powdered, dissolved in a little white brandy, and strained through fine muslin.

RATAFIA.

Pound in a mortar, and. mix together a pound of shelled bitter almonds, an ounce of nutmegs, a pound of fine loaf-sugar, and one grain (apothecaries' weight) of ambergris. Infuse these ingredients for a week in a gallon of white brandy or proof spirit. Then filter it, and bottle it for use.

CAPILLAIRE.

Powder eight pounds of loaf-sugar, and wet it with three pints of water and three eggs well beaten with their shells. Stir the whole mass very hard, and boil it twice over, skimming it well. Then strain it, and stir in two wine glasses of orange flower water. Bottle it, and use it for a summer draught, mixed with a little lemon juice and water; or you may sweeten punch with it.

ORGEAT.

To make orgeat paste, blanch, mix together, and pound in a mortar till perfectly smooth, three quarters of a pound of shelled sweet almonds, and one quarter of a pound of shelled bitter almonds; adding frequently a little orange flower or rose water, to keep them from oiling; and mixing with them, as you proceed, a pound of fine loaf-sugar that has been previously powdered by itself. When the whole is thoroughly incorporated to a stiff paste, put it into little pots and close them well. It will keep five or six months, and, when you wish to use it for a beverage, allow a piece of orgeat about the size of an egg to each half pint or tumbler of water. Having well stirred it, strain the mixture through a napkin.

To make liquid orgeat for present use; blanch and pound in a mortar, with rose water, a quarter of a pound of sweet and an ounce and a half of bitter almonds. Then sweeten three pints of rich milk with half a pound of loaf-sugar, and stir the almonds gradually into it. Boil it over hot coals; and as soon as it comes to a boil, take it off and stir it frequently till it gets cold. Then strain it, add a glass of brandy, and put it into decanters. When you pour it out for drinking dilute it with water.

LEMONADE.

Take fine ripe lemons, and roll them under your hand on the table to increase the quantity of juice. Then cut and squeeze them into a pitcher, and mix the juice with loaf-sugar and cold water. To half a pint of lemon juice you may allow a pint and a half of water; and ten or twelve moderate sized lumps of sugar. Send it round in little glasses with handles.

To make a tumbler of *very good* lemonade, allow the juice of one lemon and four or five lumps of sugar, filling up the glass with water. In summer use ice water.

ORANGEADE.

Is made of oranges, in the same proportion as lemonade. It is very fine when frozen.

PUNCH.

Roll twelve fine lemons under your hand on the table; then pare off the yellow rind very thin, and boil it in a gallon of water till all the flavour is drawn out. Break up into a large bowl, two pounds of loaf-sugar, and squeeze the lemons over it. When the water has boiled sufficiently, strain it from the lemon-peel, and mix it with the lemon juice and sugar. Stir in a quart of rum or of the best whiskey.

Two scruples of flowers of benjamin, steeped in a quart of rum, will make an infusion which much resembles the arrack of the East Indies. It should be kept in a bottle, and a little of it will be found to impart a very fine and fragrant flavour to punch made in the usual manner.

FROZEN PUNCH.

Is made as above, omitting one half of the rum or whiskey. Put it into an ice-cream freezer, shaking or stirring it all the time, when it is frozen, send it round immediately, in small glasses with a tea-spoon for each.

ROMAN PUNCH.

Grate the yellow rinds of twelve lemons and two oranges upon two pounds of loaf-sugar. Squeeze on the juice of the lemons and oranges; cover it, and let it stand till next day. Then strain it through a sieve, add a bottle of champagne, and the whites of eight eggs beaten to a froth. You may freeze it or not.

MILK PUNCH.

What is commonly called milk punch, is a mixture of brandy or rum, sugar, milk and nutmeg, with-without either lemon juice or water. It is taken cold with a lump of ice in each tumbler.

FINE MILK PUNCH.

Pare off the yellow rind of nine large lemons, and steep it for twenty-four hours in a quart of brandy or rum. Then mix with it the juice of the lemons, a pound and a half of loaf-sugar, two grated nutmegs, and a quart of water. Add a quart of rich unskimmed milk, made boiling hot, and strain the whole through a jelly-bag. You may either use it as soon as it is cold, or make a larger quantity, (in the above proportions,) and bottle it. It will keep several months.

REGENT'S PUNCH.

Take four large lemons; roll them on the table to make them more juicy, and then pare them as thin as possible. Cut out all the pulp, and throw away the seeds and the white part of the rind. Put the yellow rind and the pulp into a pint of boiling water with two tea-spoonfuls of raw green tea of the best sort. Let all boil together about ten minutes. Then strain it through linen, and stir in a pound of powdered loaf-sugar and a bottle of champagne, or of any liquor suitable for punch. Set it again over the fire, and when just ready to boil, remove it, and pour it into a china bowl or pitcher, to be sent round in glasses.

WINE JELLY.

Clarify a pound of loaf-sugar, by mixing it with half a pint of water and the beaten white of an egg, and then boiling and skimming it. Put an ounce of isinglass (with as much boiling water as will cover it) into a small sauce-pan, and set it in hot coals till the isinglass is thoroughly dissolved. Then when the syrup has been taken from the fire, mix the melted isinglass with it, add a quart of white wine and stir in a table-spoonful or a spoonful and a half of old Jamaica spirits. Stir the mixture very hard, and pour it into a mould. When it has congealed, wrap a cloth dipped in warm water round the outside of the mould; turn out the jelly, and eat it with ice-cream.

BISHOP.

The day before you want to use the liquor toast four large oranges till they are of a pale brown. You may do them either before a clear fire or in the oven of a stove. Dissolve half a pound of loaf-sugar in half a pint of claret. When the oranges are roasted, quarter them without peeling, lay them in the bottom of a bowl or a tureen, add two beaten nutmegs and some cinnamon, and pour on them the wine and sugar. Cover it, and let it stand till next day. Then having heated the remainder of the bottle of claret till it nearly boils, pour it into a pitcher, and having first pressed and mashed the pieces of orange with a spoon to bring out the juice, put them with the sugar, &c. into a cloth, and strain the liquid into the hot claret. Serve it warm in large glasses.

MULLED WINE.

Boil together in a pint of water two beaten nutmegs, a handful of broken cinnamon, and a handful of cloves slightly pounded. When the liquid is reduced to one half, strain it into a quart of port wine, which must be set on hot coals, and taken off as soon as it comes to a boil. Serve it up hot in a pitcher with little glass cups round it, and a plate of fresh rusk.

MULLED CIDER.

Allow six eggs to a quart of cider. Put a handful of whole cloves into the cider, and boil it. While it is boiling, beat the eggs in a large pitcher; adding to them as much sugar as will make the cider very sweet. By the time the cider boils, the eggs will be sufficiently light. Pour the boiling liquor on the beaten egg, and continue to pour the mixture backwards and forwards from one pitcher to another, till it has a fine froth on it. Then pour it warm into your glasses, and grate some nutmeg over each.

Port wine may be mulled in the same manner.

EGG NOGG.

Beat separately the yolks and whites of six eggs. Stir the yolks into a quart of rich milk, or thin cream, and add half a pound of sugar. Then mix in half a pint of rum or brandy. Flavour it with a grated nutmeg. Lastly, stir in gently the beaten white of an egg.

It should be mixed in a china bowl.

SANGAREE.

Mix in a pitcher or in tumblers one-third of wine, ale, or porter, with two-thirds of water either warm or cold. Stir in sufficient loaf-sugar to sweeten it, and grate some nutmeg into it.

By adding to it lemon juice, you may make what is called negus.

TURKISH SHERBET.

Having washed a fore-quarter or knuckle of veal, and cracked the bones, put it on to boil with two quarts and a pint of water. Let it boil till the liquid is reduced to one quart, and skim it well. Then strain it, and set it away to cool. When quite cold, mix with it a pint and a half of clear lemon juice, and a pint and a half of capillaire or clear sugar-syrup. If you have no capillaire ready, boil two pounds of loaf-sugar in a pint and a half of water, clearing it with the beaten white of an egg mixed into the sugar and water before boiling. Serve the sherbet cold or iced, in glass mugs at the dessert, or offer it as a refreshment at any other time.

Sherbet may be made of the juice of various sorts of fruit.

BOTTLED SMALL BEER.

Take a quart bottle of the very best brisk porter, and mix it with four quarts of water, a pint of molasses, and a table-spoonful of ginger. Bottle it, and see that the corks are of the very best kind. It will be fit for use in three or four days.

TO KEEP LEMON JUICE.

Powder a pound of the best loaf-sugar; put it into a bowl, and strain over it a pint of lemon juice; stirring it well with a silver spoon till the sugar has entirely melted. Then bottle it, sealing the corks; and keep it in a dry place.

ESSENCE OF LEMON-PEEL.

Rub lumps of loaf-sugar on fine ripe lemons till the yellow rind is all grated off; scraping up the sugar in a tea-spoon, and putting it on a plate as you proceed. When you have enough, press it down into a little glass or china jar, and cover it closely. This will be found very fine to flavour puddings and cakes.

Prepare essence of orange-peel in the same manner.

CIDER VINEGAR.

Take six quarts of rye meal; stir and mix it well into a barrel of strong hard cider of the best kind; and then add a gallon of whiskey. Cover the cask, (leaving the bung loosely in it,) set it in the part of your yard that is most exposed to the sun and air; and in the course of four weeks (if the weather is warm and dry) you will have good vinegar fit for use. When you draw off a gallon or more, replenish the cask with the same quantity of cider, and add about a pint of whiskey. You may thus have vinegar constantly at hand for common purposes.

The cask should have iron hoops.

A very strong vinegar may be made by mixing cider and strained honey, (allowing a pound of honey to a gallon of cider,) and letting it stand five or six months. This vinegar is so powerful that for common purposes it should be diluted with a little water.

Vinegar may be made in the same manner of sour wine.

WHITE VINEGAR.

Put into a cask a mixture composed of five gallons of water, two gallons of whiskey, and a quart of strong yeast, stirring in two pounds of powdered charcoal. Place it where it will ferment properly, leaving the bung loose till the fermentation is over, but covering the hole slightly to keep out the dust and insects. At the end of four months draw it off, and you will have a fine vinegar, as clear and colourless as water.

SUGAR VINEGAR.

To every gallon of water allow a pound of the best brown sugar, and a jill or more of strong yeast. Mix the sugar and water together, and boil and skim it till the scum ceases to rise. Then pour it into a tub; and when it cools to lukewarm heat, put into it the yeast spread on pieces of toast. Let it work two days; then put it into an iron-hooped cask, and set it in a sunny place for five months, leaving the bung loose, but keeping the bung-hole covered. In five months it will be good clear vinegar, and you may bottle it for use.

A cask that has not contained vinegar before, should have a quart of boiling hot vinegar poured into it, shaken about frequently till cold, and allowed to stand some hours.

PREPARATIONS FOR THE SICK.

CHICKEN JELLY.

Take a large chicken, cut it up into very small pieces, bruise the bones, and put the whole into a stone jar with a cover that will make it water tight. Set the jar in a large kettle of boiling water, and keep it boiling for three hours. Then strain off the liquid, and season it slightly with salt, pepper, and mace; or with loaf-sugar and lemon juice, according to the taste of the person for whom it is intended.

Return the fragments of the chicken to the jar, and set it again in a kettle of boiling water. You will find that you can collect nearly as much jelly by the second boiling.

This jelly may be made of an old fowl.

BREAD JELLY.

Measure a quart of boiling water, and set it away to get cold. Take one-third of a six cent loaf of bread, slice it, pare off the crust, and toast the crumb nicely of a light brown. Then put it into the boiled water, set it on hot coals in a covered pan, and boil it gently, till you find by putting some in a spoon to cool, that the liquid has become a jelly. Strain it through a thin cloth, and set it away for use. When it is to be taken, warm a tea-cupful, sweeten it with sugar, and add a little grated lemon-peel.

ARROW ROOT JELLY.

Mix three table-spoonfuls of arrow root powder in a tea-cup of water till quite smooth, cover it, and let it stand a quarter of an hour. Put the yellow peel of a lemon into a skillet with a pint of water, and let it boil till reduced to one half. Then take out the lemon-peel, and pour in the dissolved arrow root, (while the water is still boiling;) add sufficient white sugar to sweeten it well, and let it boil together for five or six minutes. It may be seasoned (if thought necessary) with two tea-spoonfuls of wine, and some grated nutmeg.

It may be boiled in milk instead of water, or in wine and water, according to the state of the person for whom it is wanted.

RICE JELLY.

Having picked and washed a quarter of a pound of rice, mix it with half a pound of loaf-sugar, and just sufficient water to cover it. Boil it till it becomes a glutinous mass; then strain it; season it with whatever may be thought proper; and let it stand to cool.

PORT WINE JELLY.

Melt in a little warm water an ounce of isinglass; stir it into a pint of port wine, adding two ounces of sugar candy, an ounce of gum arabic, and half a nutmeg grated. Mix all well, and boil it ten minutes; or till every thing is thoroughly dissolved. Then strain it through muslin, and set it away to get cold.

SAGO.

Wash the sago through two or three water, and then let it soak for two or three hours. To a tea-cupful of sago allow a quart of water and some of the yellow peel of a lemon. Simmer it till all the grains look transparent. Then add as much wine and nutmeg as may be proper, and give it another boil altogether. If seasoning is not advisable, the sago may be boiled in milk instead of water, and eaten plain.

TAPIOCA.

Wash the tapioca well, and let it steep for five or six hours, changing the water three times. Simmer it in the last water till quite clear, then season it with sugar and wine, or lemon juice.

GRUEL.

Allow three large table-spoonfuls of oatmeal or Indian meal to a quart of water. Put the meal into a large bowl, and add the water, a little at a time, mixing and bruising the meal with the back of a spoon. As you proceed, pour off the liquid into another bowl, every time, before adding fresh water to the meal, till you have used it all up. Then boil the mixture for twenty minutes, stirring it all the while; add a little salt. Then strain the gruel and sweeten it. A piece of butter may be stirred into it; and, if thought proper, a little wine and nutmeg. It should be taken warm.

OATMEAL GRUEL.

Put four table-spoonfuls of the best grits (oatmeal coarsely ground) into a pint of boiling water. Let it boil gently, and stir it often, till it becomes as thick as you wish it. Then strain it, and add to it while warm, butter, wine, nutmeg, or whatever is thought proper to flavour it.

If you make the gruel of fine oatmeal, sift it, mix it first to a thick batter with a little cold water, and then put it into the sauce-pan of boiling water. Stir it all the time it is boiling, lifting the spoon gently up and down, and letting the gruel fall slowly back again into the pan.

PANADA.

Having pared off the crust, boil some slices of bread in a quart of water for about five minutes. Then take out the bread, and beat it smooth in a deep dish, mixing in a little of the water it has boiled in; and mix it with a bit of fresh butter, and sugar and nutmeg to your taste. Another way is to grate some bread, or to grate or pound a few crackers. Pour on boiling water, beat it well, and add sugar and nutmeg.

BARLEY WATER.

Wash clean some barley, (either pearl or common) and to two ounces of barley allow a quart of water. Put it into a sauce-pan, adding, if you choose, an equal quantity of stoned raisins; or some lemon-peel and sugar; or some liquorice root cut up. Let it boil slowly till the liquid is reduced one half. Then strain it off, and sweeten it.

GROUND RICE MILK.

Mix in a bowl two table-spoonfuls of ground rice, with sufficient milk to make a thin batter. Then stir it gradually into a pint of milk and boil it with sugar, lemon-peel or nutmeg.

BEEF TEA.

Cut a pound of the lean of fresh juicy beef into small thin slices, and sprinkle them with a very little salt. Put the meat into a wide-mouthed glass or stone jar closely corked, and set it in a kettle or pan of water, which must be made to boil, and kept boiling hard round the jar for an hour or more. Then take out the jar and strain the essence of the beef into a bowl. Chicken tea may be made in the same manner.

MUTTON BROTH.

Cut off all the fat from a loin of mutton, and to each pound of the lean allow a quart of water. Season it with a little salt and some shred parsley, and put in some large pieces of the crust of bread. Boil it slowly for two or three hours, skimming it carefully.

Beef, veal, or chicken broth may be made in the same manner.

Vegetables may be added if approved. Also barley or rice.

MUTTON BROTH MADE QUICKLY.

Cut three chops from the best part of a neck of mutton, and remove the fat and skin. Beat the meat on both sides and slice it thin. Put into a small sauce-pan with a pint of water, a little salt, and some crust of bread cut into pieces. You may add a little parsley, and a small onion sliced thin. Cover the sauce-pan, and set it over the fire. Boil it fast, skim it, and in half an hour it should be ready for use.

WINE WHEY.

Boil a pint of milk; and when it rises to the top of the sauce-pan, pour in a large glass of sherry or Madeira. It will be the better for adding a glass of currant wine also. Let it again boil up, and then take the sauce-pan off the fire, and set it aside to stand for a few minutes, but do not stir it. Then remove the curd, (if it has completely formed,) and pour the clear whey into a bowl and sweeten it.

When wine is considered too heating, the whey may be made by turning the milk with lemon juice.

RENNET WHEY.

Wash a small bit of rennet about two inches square, in cold water, to get off the salt. Put it into a tea-cup and pour on it sufficient lukewarm water to cover it. Let it stand all night, and in the morning stir the rennet water into a quart pitcher of warm milk. Cover it, and set it near the fire till a firm curd is formed. Pour off the whey from it, and it will be found an excellent and cooling drink. The curd may be eaten (though not by a sick person) with wine, sugar, and nutmeg.

CALF'S FEET BROTH.

Boil two calf's feet in two quarts of water, till the liquid is reduced one half, and the meat has dropped to pieces. Then strain it into a deep dish or pan, and set it by to get cold. When it has congealed, take all the fat carefully off; put a tea-cupful of the jelly into a sauce-pan, and set it on hot coals. When it has nearly boiled, stir in by degrees the beaten yolk of an egg, and then take it off immediately. You may add to it a little sugar, and some grated lemon-peel and nutmeg.

CHICKEN BROTH AND PANADA.

Cut up a chicken, season it with a very little salt, and put it into three quarts of water. Let it simmer slowly till the flesh drops to pieces. You may make chicken panada or gruel of the same fowl, by taking out the white meat as soon as it is tender, mincing it fine, and then pounding it in a mortar, adding as you pound it, sufficient of the chicken water to moisten the paste. You may thin it with water till it becomes liquid enough to drink. Then put it into a sauce-pan and boil it gently a few minutes. Taken in small quantities, it will be found very nutritious. You may add to it a little grated lemon-peel and nutmeg.

VEGETABLE SOUP.

Take a white onion, a turnip, a pared potato, and a head of celery, or a large tea-spoonful of celery seed. Put the vegetables whole into a quart of water, (adding a little salt,) and boil it slowly till reduced to a pint. Make a slice of nice toast; lay it in the bottom of a bowl, and strain the soup over it.

ONION SOUP.

Put half a pound of the best fresh butter into a stew-pan on the fire, and let it boil till it has done making a noise; then have ready twelve large onions peeled and cut small; throw them into the butter, add a little salt, and stew them a quarter of an hour. Then dredge in a little flour, and stir the whole very hard; and in five minutes pour in a quart of boiling water, and some of the upper crust of bread, cut small. Let the soup boil ten minutes longer, stirring it often; and after you take it from the fire, stir in the yolks of two beaten eggs, and serve it up immediately,

In France this soup is considered a fine restorative after any unusual fatigue. Instead of butter, the onions may be boiled in veal or chicken broth.

TOAST AND WATER.

Toast some slices of bread very nicely, without allowing them to burn or blacken. Then put them into a pitcher, and fill it up with boiling water. Let it stand till it is quite cold; then strain it, and put it into a decanter. Another way of preparing toast and water is to put the toasted bread into a mug and pour cold water on it. Cover it closely, and let it infuse for at least an hour. Drink it cold.

APPLE WATER.

Pare and slice a fine juicy apple; pour boiling water over it, cover it, and let it stand till cold.

TAMARIND WATER.

Put tamarinds into a pitcher or tumbler till it is one-third full; then fill it up with cold water, cover it, and let it infuse for a quarter of an hour or more.

Currant jelly or cranberry juice mixed with water makes a pleasant drink for an invalid.

MOLASSES POSSETS.

Put into a sauce-pan a pint of the best West India molasses; a tea-spoonful of powdered white ginger; and a quarter of a pound of fresh butter. Set it on hot coals, and simmer it slowly for half an hour; stirring it frequently. Do not let it come to a boil. Then stir in the juice of two lemons, or two table-spoonfuls of vinegar; cover the pan, and let it stand by the fire five minutes longer. This is good for a cold. Some of it may be taken warm at once, and the remainder kept at hand for occasional use.

It is the preparation absurdly called by the common people a stewed quaker.

Half a pint of strained honey mixed cold with the juice of a lemon, and a table-spoonful of sweet oil, is another remedy for a cold; a tea-spoonful or two to be taken whenever the cough is troublesome.

FLAX-SEED LEMONADE.

To a large table-spoonful of flax-seed allow a tumbler and a half of cold water. Boil them together till the liquid becomes very sticky. Then strain it hot over a quarter of a pound of pulverized sugar candy, and an ounce of pulverized gum arabic. Stir it till quite dissolved, and squeeze into it the juice of a lemon.

This mixture has frequently been found an efficacious remedy for a cold; taking a wine-glass of it as often as the cough is troublesome.

COCOA.

Put into a sauce-pan two ounces of good cocoa (the chocolate nut before it is ground) and one quart of water. Cover it, and as soon as it has come to a boil, set it on coals by the side of the fire, to simmer for an hour or more. Take it hot with dry toast.

COCOA SHELLS.

These can be procured at the principal grocers and confectioners, or at a chocolate manufactory. They are the thin shells that envelope the chocolate kernel, and are sold at a low price; a pound contains a very large quantity. Soak them in water for five or six hours or more, (it will be better to soak them all night,) and then boil them in the same water. They should boil two hours. Strain the liquid when done, and let it be taken warm.

RAW EGG.

Break a fresh egg into a saucer, and mix a little sugar with it; also, if approved, a small quantity of wine. Beat the whole to a strong froth. It is considered a restorative.

SODA WATER.

To forty grains of carbonate of soda, add thirty grains of tartaric acid in small crystals. Fill a soda bottle with spring water, put in the mixture, and cork it instantly with a well-fitting cork.

SEIDLITZ POWDERS.

Fold in a white paper one drachm of Rochelle salts. In a blue paper a mixture of twenty grains of tartaric acid, and twenty-five grains of carbonate of soda. They should all be pulverized very fine. Put the contents of the white paper into a tumbler not quite half full of cold water, and stir it till dissolved. Then put the mixture from the blue paper into another tumbler with the same quantity of water, and stir that also. When the powders are dissolved in both tumblers, pour the first into the other, and it will effervesce immediately. Drink it quickly while foaming.

BITTERS.

Take two ounces of gentian root, an ounce of Virginia snake root, an ounce of the yellow paring of orange peel, and half a drachm of cochineal. Steep these ingredients, for a week or more, in a quart of Madeira or sherry wine, or brandy. When they are thoroughly infused, strain and filter the liquor, and bottle it for use. This is considered a good tonic, taken in a small cordial glass about noon.

ESSENCE OF PEPPERMINT.

Mix an ounce of oil of peppermint with a pint of alcohol. Then colour it by putting in some leaves of green mint. Let it stand till the colour is a fine green; then filter it through blotting paper. Drop it on sugar when you take it.

Essence of pennyroyal, mint, cinnamon, cloves, &c. may all be prepared in the same manner by mixing a portion of the essential oil with a little alcohol.

You may obtain liquid camphor by breaking up and dissolving a lump in white brandy or spirit of wine.

LAVENDER COMPOUND.

Fill a quart bottle with lavender blossoms freshly gathered, and put in loosely; then pour in as much of the best brandy as it will contain. Let it stand a fortnight, and then strain it. Afterwards, mix with it of powdered cloves, mace, nutmeg and cochineal, a quarter of an ounce of each; and cork it up for use in small bottles. When taken, a little should be dropped on a lump of sugar.

LEAD WATER.

Mix two table-spoonfuls of extract of lead with a bottle of rain or river water. Then add two table-spoonfuls of brandy, and shake it well.

[Footnote: These remedies are all very simple; but the author *knows* them to have been efficacious whenever tried.]

REMEDY FOR A BURN.

After immediately applying sweet oil, scrape the inside of a raw potato, and lay some of it on the place, securing it with a rag. In a short time put on fresh potato, and repeat this application very frequently. It will give immediate ease, and draw out the fire. Of course, if the burn is bad, it is best to send for a physician.

FOR CHILBLAINS.

Dip the feet every night and morning in cold water, withdrawing them in a minute or two, and drying them by rubbing them very hard with a coarse towel. To put them immediately into a pail of brine brought from a pickle tub is another excellent remedy when feet are found to be frosted.

FOR CORNS.

Mix together a little Indian meal and cold water, till it is about the consistence of thick mush. Then bind it on the corn by wrapping a small slip of thin rag round the toe. It will not prevent you from wearing your shoe and stocking. In two or three hours take it off, and you will find the corn much softened. Cut off as much of it as is soft with a penknife or scissors. Then put on a fresh poultice, and repeat it till the corn is entirely levelled, as it will be after a few regular applications of the remedy; which will be found successful whenever the corn returns. There is no permanent cure for them.

WARTS.

To remove the hard callous horny warts which sometimes appear on the hands of children, touch the wart carefully with a new pen dipped slightly in aqua-fortis. It will give no pain; and after repeating it a few times, the wart will be found so loose as to come off by rubbing it with the finger.

RING-WORMS.

Rub mercurial ointment on the ring-worm previous to going to bed, and do not wash it off till morning. It will effect a cure if persevered in; sometimes in less than a week.

MUSQUITO BITES.

Salt wetted into a sort of paste, with a little vinegar, and plastered on the bite, will immediately allay the pain; and if not rubbed, no mark will be seen next day. It is well to keep salt and vinegar always in a chamber that is infested with musquitoes. It is also good for the sting of a wasp or bee; and for the bite of any venomous animal, if applied immediately. It should be left on till it becomes dry, and then renewed.

ANTIDOTE FOR LAUDANUM.

When so large a quantity of laudanum has been swallowed as to produce dangerous effects, the fatal drowsiness has been prevented when all other remedies have failed, by administering a cup of the strongest possible coffee. The patient has revived and recovered, and no ill effects have followed.

GREEN OINTMENT.

Take two or three large handfuls of the fresh-gathered leaves of the Jamestown weed, (called Apple Peru in New England,) and pound it in a mortar till you have extracted the juice. Then put the juice into a tin sauce-pan, mixed with sufficient lard to make a thick salve. Stew them together ten or fifteen minutes, and then pour the mixture into gallipots and cover it closely. It is excellent to rub on chilblains, and other inflammatory external swellings, applying it several times a day.

TO STOP BLOOD.

For a prick with a pin, or a slight cut, nothing will more effectually stop the bleeding than old cobwebs compressed into a lump and applied to the wound, or bound on it with a rag. A scrap of cotton wadding is also good for stopping blood.

PERFUMERY, ETC.

COLOGNE WATER.

Procure at a druggists, one drachm of oil of lavender, the same quantity of oil of lemon, of oil of rosemary, and of oil of cinnamon; with two drachms of oil of bergamot, all mixed in the same phial, which should be a new one. Shake the oils well, and pour them into a pint of spirits of wine. Cork the bottle tightly, shake it hard, and it will be fit for immediate use; though it improves by keeping. You may add to the oils, if you choose, ten drops of the tincture of musk, or ten drops of extract of ambergris.

For very fine cologne water, mix together in a new phial oil of lemon, two drachms; oil of bergamot, two drachms; oil of lavender, two drachms; oil of cedrat, one drachm; tincture of benzoin, three drachms; neroli, ten drops; ambergris, ten drops; attar of roses, two drops. Pour the mixture into a pint of spirits of wine; cork and shake the bottle, and set it away for use.

Another receipt for cologne water is to mix with a pint of alcohol, sixty drops or two large tea-spoonfuls of orange-flower water, and the same quantity of the essential oils of lemon, lavender, and bergamot.

LAVENDER WATER.

Mix two ounces of essential oil of lavender, and two drachms of essence of ambergris, with a pint of spirits of wine; cork the bottle, and shake it hard every day for a fortnight.

HUNGARY WATER.

Mix together one ounce of oil of rosemary and two drachms of essence of ambergris; add them to a pint of spirits of wine. Shake it daily for a month, and then transfer it to small bottles.

ROSE VINEGAR.

Fill a stone or china jar with fresh rose leaves put in loosely. Then pour on them as much of the best white wine vinegar as the jar will hold. Cover it, and set it in the sun, or in some other warm place for three weeks. Then strain it through a flannel bag, and bottle it for use, This vinegar will he found very fine for salads, or for any nice purposes.

THIEVES' VINEGAR.

Take a large handful of lavender blossoms, and the same quantity of sage, mint, rue, wormwood and rosemary. Chop and mix them well. Put them into a jar, with half an ounce of camphor that has been dissolved in a little alcohol, and pour in three quarts of strong clear vinegar. Keep the jar for two or three weeks in the hot sun, and at night plunge it into a box of heated sand. Afterwards strain and bottle the liquid, putting into each bottle a clove of garlic sliced. To have it very clear, after it has been bottled for a week, you should pour it off carefully from the sediment, and filter it through blotting paper. Then wash the bottles, and return the vinegar to them. It should be kept very tightly corked. It is used for sprinkling about in sick-rooms; and also in close damp oppressive weather. Inhaling the odour from a small bottle will frequently prevent faintness in a crowd.

It is best to make it in June.

This vinegar is so called from an old tradition, that during the prevalence of the plague in London the composition was invented by four thieves, who found it a preservative from contagion; and were by that means enabled to remain in the city and exercise their profession to great advantage, after most of the inhabitants had fled.

OIL OF FLOWERS.

A French process for obtaining essential oils from flowers or herbs has been described as follows:—Take carded cotton, or split wadding and steep it in some pure Florence oil, such as is quite clear and has no smell. Then place a layer of this cotton in the bottom of a deep china dish, or in an earthen pipkin. Cover it with a thick layer of fresh rose leaves, or the leaves of sweet pink, jasmine, wall-flower, tuberose, magnolia blossoms, or any other odoriferous flower or plant from which you wish to obtain the perfume. Spread over the flower-leaves another layer of cotton that has been steeped in oil. Afterwards a second layer of flowers, and repeat them alternately till the vessel is quite full. Cover it closely, and let it stand in the sun for a week. Then throw away the flower-leaves, carefully press out the oil from the cotton, and put it into a small bottle for use. The oil will be found to have imbibed the odour of the flowers.

Keep the scented cotton to perfume your clothes-presses.

BALM OF GILEAD OIL.

Put loosely into a bottle as many balm of Gilead flowers as will come up to a third part of its height; then nearly fill up the bottle with sweet oil, which should be of the best quality. Let it infuse (shaking it occasionally) for several days, and it will then be fit for use. It is considered a good remedy for bruises of the skin; also for cuts, burns, and scalds that are not very bad, and should be applied immediately,—by wetting a soft rag with it; renewing it frequently,

LIP SALVE.

Put into a wide-mouthed bottle four ounces of the best olive oil, with one ounce of the small parts of alkanet root. Stop up the bottle, and set it in the sun, (shaking it often,) till you find the liquid of a beautiful crimson. Then strain off the oil very clear from the alkanet root, put it into an earthen pipkin, and add to it an ounce of white wax, and an ounce and a half of the best mutton suet, which has been previously clarified, or boiled and skimmed. Set the mixture on the embers of coals, and melt it slowly: stirring it well. After it has simmered slowly far a little while, take it off; and while still hot, mix with it a few drops of oil of roses, or of oil of neroli, or tincture of musk.

COLD CREAM.

Cut very fine a drachm of white wax and a drachm of spermaceti. Put it into a small sauce-pan with one ounce of oil of sweet almonds, and mix them well together. Set it on hot coals, and as soon as it has boiled take it off, and stir in an ounce of orange-flower or rose-water. Beat it very hard, and then put it into gallipots.

SOFT POMATUM.

Soak half a pound of fresh lard and a quarter of a pound of beef marrow in water for two or three days; squeezing and pressing it every day, and changing the water. Afterwards drain off the water, and put the lard and marrow into a sieve to dry. Then transfer it to a jar, and set the jar into a pot of boiling water. When the mixture is melted, put it into a basin, and beat it with two spoonfuls of brandy. Then drain off the brandy, perfume the pomatum by mixing with it any scented essence that you please, and tie it up in gallipots.

COSMETIC PASTE.

Take a quarter of a pound of Castile soap, and cut it into small pieces. Then, put it into a tin or porcelain sauce-pan, with just water enough to moisten it well, and set it on hot coals. Let it simmer till it is entirely dissolved; stirring it till it becomes a smooth paste, and thickening it with Indian meal, (which even in a raw state is excellent for the hands.) Then take it from the fire, and when cool scent it with rose-water, or with any fragrant essence you please. Beat and stir it hard with a silver spoon, and when it is thoroughly mixed put it into little pots with covers.

ACID SALT.

This is the composition commonly, but erroneously called salt of lemon, and is excellent for removing ink and other stains from the hands, and for taking ink spots out of white clothes. Pound together in a marble mortar an ounce of salt of sorrel, and an ounce of the best cream of tartar, mixing them thoroughly. Then, put it in little wooden boxes or covered gallipots, and rub it on your hands when they are stained, washing them in cold water, and using the acid salt instead of soap; a very small quantity will immediately remove the stain. In applying it to linen or muslin that is spotted with ink or fruit juice, hold the stained part tightly stretched over a cup or bowl of boiling water. Then with your finger rub on the acid salt till the stain disappears. It must always be done before the article is washed.

This mixture costs about twenty-five cents, and the above quantity (if kept dry) will be sufficient for a year or more.

Ink stains may frequently be taken out of white clothes by rubbing on (before they go to the wash) some bits of cold tallow picked from the bottom of a mould candle; Leave the tallow sticking on in a lump, and when the article comes from the wash, it will generally be found that the spot has disappeared. This experiment is so easy and so generally successful that it is always worth trying. When it fails, it is in consequence of some peculiarity in the composition of the ink.

SWEET JARS.

Take a china jar, and put into it three handfuls of fresh damask rose-leaves; three of sweet pinks, three of wall-flowers, and stock gilly-flowers, and equal proportions of any other fragrant flowers that you can procure. Place them in layers; strewing fine salt thickly between each layer, and mixing with them an ounce of sliced orris root.

You may fill another jar with equal quantities of lavender, knotted marjoram, rosemary, lemon thyme, balm of Gilead, lemon-peel, and smaller quantities of laurel leaves and mint; and some sliced orris root. You may mix with the herbs, (which must all be chopped,) cloves, cinnamon, and sliced nutmeg; strewing salt between the layers.

Flowers, herbs, and spice may all be mixed in the same jar; adding always some orris root. Every thing that is put in should be perfectly free from damp.

The jar should be kept closely covered, except when the cover is occasionally removed for the purpose of diffusing the scent through the room.

SCENTED BAGS.

Take a quarter of a pound of coriander seeds, a quarter of a pound of orris root, a quarter of a pound of aromatic calamus, a quarter of a pound of damask rose leaves, two ounces of lavender blossoms, half an ounce of mace, half an ounce of cinnamon, a quarter of an ounce of cloves, and two drachms of musk-powder. Beat them all separately in a mortar, and then mix them well together. Make small silk or satin bags; fill each with a portion of the mixture, and sew them closely all round. Lay them among your clothes in the drawers.

VIOLET PERFUME.

Drop twelve drops of genuine oil of rhodium on a lump of loaf-sugar. Then pound the sugar in a marble mortar with two ounces of orris root powder. This will afford an excellent imitation of the scent of violets. If you add more oil of rhodium, it will produce a rose perfume. Sew up the powder in little silk bags, or keep it in a tight box.

DURABLE INK.

Take, when empty, one of the little bottles that has contained indelible ink, such as is sold in cases, and wash and rinse it clean. Put into it half an inch of lunar caustic; fill it up with good vinegar, and cork it tightly. This is the marking ink.

Prepare the larger bottle that has contained the liquid used for the first wash, by making it quite clean. Take a large tea-spoonful of salt of tartar, and a lump of gum arabic the size of a hickory nut. Put them into the wash bottle, and fill it up with clear rain water, Cork both bottles tightly, and set them for two days in the sun. The liquids will then be fit for use.

Linen cannot be marked well with durable ink unless the weather is clear and dry. Dip a camel's hair pencil in the large bottle that contains the gum liquid, and wash over with it a small space on a corner of the linen, about large enough to contain the name. Dry it in the sun, and let it alone till next day. Then take a very good pen, acid with the ink from the smallest bottle, write the name you intend, on the place that has been prepared by the first liquid. This also must be dried in the sun. See that the bottles are always well corked, and keep them in a covered box.

After the linen is dried, iron it before you write on it.

ANOTHER DURABLE INK.

For the marking liquid—rub together in a small mortar five scruples of lunar caustic with one drachm of gum arabic, one scruple of sap-green and one ounce of rain water.

For wetting the linen—mix together one ounce of salt of soda, two ounces of boiling water, and a table-spoonful of powdered gum arabic.

TO KEEP PEARL-ASH.

Take three ounces of pearl-ash, and put it into a clean black bottle with a pint and a half (not more) of soft water. The proportion is an ounce of pearl-ash to half a pint of water. Cork it very tightly, shake it, and it will be fit for use as soon as all the pearl-ash is dissolved. A table-spoonful of this liquid is equal to a small tea-spoonful of pearl-ash in the lump or powder. Keeping it ready dissolved will be found very convenient.

ALMOND PASTE.

Blanch half a pound of shelled sweet, almonds, and a quarter of a pound of bitter ones, and beat them in a mortar to a smooth paste—adding by degrees a jill of rose or orange-flower water. Then beat in, gradually, half a pound of clear strained honey. When the whole is well incorporated, put it into gallipots, pouring on the top of each some orange-flower or rose-water. Keep it closely covered. This is a celebrated cosmetic for the hands.

MISCELLANEOUS RECEIPTS.

MINCED OYSTERS.

Take fifty fine large oysters, and mince them raw. Chop also four or five small pickled cucumbers, and a bunch of parsley. Grate about two tea-cupfuls of stale bread-crumbs, and beat up the yolks of four eggs. Mix the whole together in a thick batter, seasoning it with cayenne and powdered mace; and with a little salt if the oysters are fresh. Have ready a pound of lard, and melt in the frying-pan enough of it to fry the oysters well. If the lard is in too small a quantity they will be flat and tough. When the lard is boiling hot in the pan, put in about a table-spoonful at a time of the oyster-mixture, and fry it in the form of small fritters; turning them so as to brown on both sides. Serve them up hot, and eat them with small bread rolls.

STEWED BLACK FISH.

Flour a deep dish, and lay in the bottom a piece of butter rolled in flour. Then sprinkle it with a mixture of parsley, sweet marjoram, and green onion; all chopped fine. Take your black fish and rub it inside and outside with a mixture of cayenne, salt, and powdered cloves and mace. Place skewers across the dish, and lay the fish upon them. Then pour in a little wine, and sufficient water to stew the fish. Set the dish in a moderate oven, and let it cook slowly for an hour.

Shad or rock fish may be dressed in the same manner.

FRIED SMELTS.

These little fish are considered extremely fine. Before they are cooked, cut off the heads and tails. Sprinkle the smelts with flour, and have ready in a frying pan over the fire plenty of fresh lard or butter. When it boils, put in the fish and fry them.

BROILED SWEET-BREADS.

Split open and skewer the sweet-breads; season them with pepper and salt, and with powdered mace. Broil them on a gridiron till thoroughly done. While they are broiling, prepare some melted butter seasoned with mace and a little white wine, or mushroom catchup; and have ready some toast with the crust cut off. Lay the toast in the bottom of a dish; place the sweet-breads upon it, and pour over them the drawn butter.

PICKLED EGGS.

Boil twelve eggs quite hard, and lay them in cold water; having peeled off the shells. Then put them whole into a stone jar, with a quarter of an ounce of whole mace, and the same quantity of cloves; a sliced nutmeg; a table-spoonful of whole pepper; a small bit of ginger; and a peach leaf. Fill up the jar with boiling vinegar; cover it closely that the eggs may cool slowly. When they are cold, tie up the jar; covering the cork with leather. After it has stood three days pour off the pickle, boil it up again, and return it boiling hot to the eggs and spice. They will be fit for use in a fortnight.

GUMBO SOUP.

Take four pounds of the lean of a fresh round of beef and cut the meat into small pieces, avoiding carefully all the fat. Season the meat with a little pepper and salt, and put it on to boil with three quarts and a pint of water (not more.) Boil it slowly and skim it well. When no more scum rises, put in half a peck of ochras, peeled and sliced, and half a peck of tomatas cut in quarters. Boil it slowly till the ochras and tomatas are entirely dissolved, and the meat all to rags. Then strain it through a cullender, and send it to table with slices of dry toast. This soup cannot be made in less than seven or eight hours. If you dine at two, you must put on the meat to boil at six or seven in the morning. It should be as thick as a jelly.

SHREWSBURY CAKES.

Rub three quarters of a pound of butter into two pounds of sifted flour, and mix in half a pound of powdered sugar, and half a pound of currants, washed and dried. Wet it to a stiff paste with rich milk. Roll it out, and cut it into cakes. Lay them on buttered baking sheets, and put them into a moderate oven.

RICE FLUMMERY.

To two quarts of milk allow half a pound of ground rice. Take out one pint of the milk, and mix the rice gradually with it into a batter; making it quite smooth and free from lumps. Put the three pints of milk into a skillet, (with a bunch of peach leaves or a few peach-kernels,) and let it come to a boil. Then while it is still boiling, stir in by degrees the rice batter, taking care not to have it lumpy; add sugar, mace, and rose brandy to your taste; or you may flavour it with a small tea-spoonful of oil of lemon. When it has boiled sufficiently, and is quite thick, strain it, and put it into a mould to congeal. Make a rich boiled custard, (flavoured in the same manner,) and send it to table in a pitcher to eat with the flummery. Both should be cold. If you mould it in tea-cups, turn it out on a deep dish, and pour the custard round it.

APPLE BUTTER WITHOUT CIDER.

To ten gallons of water add six gallons of the best molasses, mixing them well together. Put it into a large kettle over a good fire; let it come to a hard boil, and skim it as long as any scum continues to rise. Then take out half the liquid, and put it into a tub. Have ready eight bushels of fine sound apples, pared, cored and quartered. Throw them gradually into the liquid that is still boiling on the fire. Let it continue to boil hard, and as it thickens, add by degrees the other half of the molasses and water, (that which has been put into the tub.) Stir it frequently to prevent its scorching, and to make it of equal consistence throughout. Boil it ten or twelve hours, continuing to stir it. At night take it out of the kettle, and set it in tubs to cool; covering it carefully. Wash out the kettle and wipe it very dry.

Next morning boil the apple butter six or eight hours longer; it should boil eighteen hours altogether. Half an hour before you take it finally out, stir in a pound of mixed spice; cloves, allspice, cinnamon, and nutmeg, all finely powdered. When entirely done, put up the apple butter in stone or earthen jars. It will keep a year or more.

It can, of course, be made in a smaller quantity than that given in the above receipt; and also at any time in the winter; fresh cider not being an ingredient, as in the most usual way of making apple butter.

AN APPLE POT PIE.

Make a paste, allowing a pound of butter, or of chopped suet to two pounds and a quarter of flour. Have ready a sufficient quantity of fine juicy acid apples, pared, cored, and sliced. Mix with them brown sugar enough to sweeten them, a few cloves, and some slips of lemon-peel. Butter the inside of an iron pot, and line it with some of the paste. Then put in the apples, interspersing them with thin squares of paste, and add a very little water. Cover the whole with a thick lid of the dough, which must be carefully closed round the edges. Pour on water enough to fill the pot, and let it boil two hours. When done, serve it up on a large dish, and eat it with butter and sugar.

PUDDING CATCHUP.

Mix together half a pint of noyau; a pint of sherry or other white wine; the yellow peel of four lemons, pared thin; and half an ounce of mace. Put the whole into a large bottle, and let it stand for two or three weeks. Then strain it, and add half a pint of capillaire or strong sugar syrup; or of Curaçoa. Bottle it, and it will keep two or three years. It may be used for various sweet dishes, but chiefly for pudding-sauce mixed with melted butter.

CURAÇOA.

Pound as much dried orange-peel as will make six ounces when done; the peel of fresh shaddock will be still better; or you may substitute six drachms of the oil of orange-peel. Put it into a quart of the strongest and clearest rectified spirit; shake it, let it infuse for a fortnight, and strain it. Then make a syrup by dissolving a pound of the best loaf-sugar in a pint of cold water, adding to it the beaten white of an egg, and boiling and skimming it till the scum ceases to rise. Mix the syrup with the strained liquor. Let it stand till next day, and then filter it through white blotting paper fastened to the bottom of a sieve. Curaçoa is a great improvement to punch; also a tablespoonful of it in a tumbler of water makes a very refreshing summer drink.

PATENT YEAST.

Boil half a pound of fresh hops in four quarts of water, till the liquid is reduced to two quarts Strain it, and mix in sufficient wheat flour to make a thin batter; adding half a pint of strong fresh yeast, (brewer's yeast, if it can be procured.) When it is done fermenting, pour it into a pan, and stir in sufficient Indian meal to make a moderately stiff dough. Cover it, and set it in a warm place to rise. When it has become very light, roll it out into a thick sheet, and cut it into little cakes. Spread them out on a dish, and let them dry gradually in a cool place where there is no sun. Turn them five or six times a day while drying; and when they are quite dry, put them into paper bags, and keep them in a jar or box closely covered, in a place that is not in the least damp.

When you want the yeast for use, dissolve in a little warm water one or more of the cakes, (in proportion to the quantity of bread you intend making,) and when it is quite dissolved, stir it hard, thicken it with a little flour, cover it, and place it near the fire to rise before you use it. Then mix it with the flour in the usual manner of preparing bread.

This is a very convenient way of preserving yeast through the summer, or of conveying it to a distance.

TO DRY HERBS.

By drying herbs with artificial heat as quickly as possible, you preserve their scent and flavour much better than when they are dried slowly by exposing them to the sun and air; a process by which a large portion of their strength evaporates. All sorts of herbs are in the greatest perfection just before they begin to flower. Gather them on a dry day, and place them in an oven, which must not be hot enough to discolour, scorch, or burn them. When they are quite dry, take them out, and replace them with others. Pick the leaves from, the stems, (which may be thrown away,) and put them into bottles or jars; cork them tightly, and keep them in a dry place. Those that are used in cookery should be kept in a kitchen closet.

PEACH KERNELS.

When peaches are in season, have in a convenient place an old basket or something of the sort, in which all the peach stones can be saved; they are too useful to be thrown away. Then have them carefully cracked, so as to extract the kernels whole if possible. Spread them out on a dish for one day. Then, put them into a box or jar, and keep them to use as bitter almonds; for which they are an excellent substitute in flavouring custards, creams and cakes. Plum stones are worth saving in the same manner.

LEMON-PEEL.

Never throw away the rind of a lemon; Keep a wide-mouthed bottle half full of brandy, and put into it (cut in pieces) all the lemon-rind that you do not immediately want. As the white part of the rind is of no use, it will be best to pare off the yellow very thin, and put that alone into the brandy, which will thus imbibe a very fine lemon flavour, and may be used for many nice purposes.

TO KEEP TOMATAS.

Take fine ripe tomatas, and wipe them dry, taking care not to break the skin. Put them, into a stone jar with cold vinegar, adding a small thin muslin bag filled with mace, whole cloves, and whole peppers. Then cork the jar tightly with a cork that has been dipped in melted rosin, and put it away in a dry place. Tomatas pickled in this manner keep perfectly well and retain their colour. For this purpose use the small round button tomatas.

ADDITIONAL RECEIPTS.

FRENCH GREEN PEA SOUP.

This soup is made without meat. Put into a soup-pot four quarts of shelled green peas, two large onions sliced, a handful of leaves of sweet marjoram shred from the stalks, or a handful of sweet basil; or a mixed handful of both—also, if you like it, a handful of green mint. Add four quarts of water, and boil the whole slowly till all the peas are entirely to pieces. Then take off the pot, and mash the peas well against its sides to extract from them all their flavour. Afterward strain off the liquid into a clean pot, and add to it a tea-cup full of the juice of spinach, which you must prepare, while the soup is boiling, by pounding some spinach in a mortar. This will give the soup a fine green colour. Then put in a quarter of a pound of the best fresh butter rolled whole in flour; and add a pint and a half more of shelled young peas. If you wish the soup very thick, you may allow a quart of the additional peas. Season it with a very little salt and cayenne; put it again over the fire, and boil it till the last peas are quite soft, but not till they go to pieces.

Have ready in a tureen two or three slices of toasted bread cut into small squares or dice, and pour the soup on it.

This soup, if properly made, will be found excellent, notwithstanding the absence of meat. It is convenient for fast days; and in the country, where vegetables can be obtained from the garden, the expense will be very trifling. What is left may be warmed for the next day.

GIBLET SOUP.

Take three pounds of shin of beef or of neck of mutton. Cut off the meat and break the bones. Then put the meat with the bones into a soup-pot, with a tea-spoonful of salt, and three quarts of water. Add a bunch of sweet marjoram, one of sweet basil, and a quarter of an ounce of black pepper-corns, all tied in a thin muslin rag; a sliced onion, and six or eight turnips and carrots, cut small. Let the whole boil slowly for two or three hours, skimming it well. In the meantime, have ready two sets of goose-giblets, or four of duck. They must be scalded, and well washed in warm water. Cut off the bills and split the heads; and cut the necks and gizzards into mouthfuls. Having taken the meat and bones out of the soup, put in the giblets, with a head of celery chopped. Boil it slowly an hour and a half; or more, taking care to skim it. Make a thickening of an ounce and a half of butter, and a large table-spoonful of flour, mixed together with a little of the soup. Then stir it into the pot, adding a large table-spoonful of mushroom catchup, and some small force-meat balls, or

little dumplings. Boil the soup half an hour longer. Then send it to table with the giblets in the tureen.

GUMBO.

Take an equal quantity of young tender ochras, and of ripe tomatas, (for instance, a quarter of a peck of each.) Chop the ochras fine, and scald and peel the tomatas. Put them into a stew-pan without any water. Add a lump of butter, and a very little salt and pepper; and, if you choose, an onion minced fine. Let it stew steadily for an hour. Then strain it, and send it to table as soup in a tureen. It should be like a jelly, and is a favourite New Orleans dish. Eat dry toast with it.

HAM OMELET.

Take six ounces of cold coiled ham, and mince it very fine, adding a little pepper. Beat separately the whites and yolks of six eggs, and then mix them together add to them gradually the minced ham. Beat the whole very hard, and do not let it stand a moment after it is thoroughly mixed. Have ready some boiling lard in a frying-pan, and put in the omelet immediately. Fry it about ten minutes or a quarter of an hour. When done, put it on a hot dish, trim off the edges, and fold it over in a half moon. Send it to table hot, and covered. It is eaten at breakfast.

If you wish a soft omelet, (not to fold over,) fry it a shorter time, and serve it in a deep dish, to be helped with a spoon.

A similar omelet may be made of the lean of a cold smoked tongue.

BATTER PUDDING.

Take a quart of milk, and stir into it gradually eight table spoonfuls of sifted flour, carefully pressing out all the lumps with the back of the spoon. Beat eight eggs very light, and add them by degrees to the milk and flour. Then stir the whole very well together.

Dip your pudding-cloth into boiling water, and then dredge it with flour. Pour in the pudding, and tie it tightly, leaving room for it to swell. Put it into a pot full of boiling water, and boil it hard for two hours. Keep it in the pot till it is time to send it to table. Serve it up with wine-sauce, butter and sugar, or molasses and cold butter.

PEACH MANGOES.

Take free-stone peaches of the largest size, (when they are full grown, but not quite ripe,) and lay them in salt and water for two days, covered with a board to keep them down. Then take them out, wipe them dry, cut them open, and extract the stones. Mix together, to your taste, minced garlic, scraped horseradish, bruised mustard seed, and cloves; and a little ginger-root soaked in water to soften, and then sliced. Fill the cavity of the peaches with this mixture. Then tie them round with packthread, and put them into a stone jar till it is two-thirds full. Strew among them some whole cloves, broken cinnamon, and a little cochineal. Season some cold vinegar, (allowing to each quart a jill of fresh made mustard, and a little ginger, and nutmeg,) and having mixed this pickle well, fill up the jar with it.

BROILED TOMATAS.

Take large ripe tomatas; wipe them, and split them in half. Broil them on a gridiron till brown, turning them when half done. Have ready in a dish some butter seasoned with a little pepper. When the tomatas are well broiled, put them into the dish, and press each a little with the back of a spoon, so that the juice may run into the butter and mix with it. This is to make the gravy. Send them to table hot.

Tomatas are very good sliced, and fried in butter.

PRESERVED TOMATAS.

Take large fine tomatas, (not too ripe,) and scald them to make the skins come off easily. Weigh them, and to each pound allow a pound of the best brown sugar, and the grated peel of a large lemon. Put all together into a preserving kettle, and having boiled it slowly for three hours, (skimming it carefully,) add the juice of the lemons, and boil it an hour longer. Then put the whole into jars, and when cool cover and tie them up closely. This is a cheap and excellent sweetmeat; but the lemon must on no account be omitted. It may be improved by boiling a little ginger with the other ingredients.

TOMATA HONEY.

To each pound of tomatas, allow the grated peel of a lemon and six fresh peach-leaves. Boil them slowly till they are all to pieces; then squeeze and strain them through a bag. To each pint of liquid allow a pound of loaf-sugar, and the juice of one lemon. Boil them together half an hour, or till they become a thick jelly. Then put it into glasses, and lay double tissue paper closely over the top. It will be scarcely distinguishable from real honey.

PRESERVED CUCUMBERS.

Your cucumbers should be well shaped, and all of the same size. Spread the bottom and sides of a preserving kettle with a thick layer of vine leaves. Then put in the cucumbers—with a little alum broken small. Cover them thickly with vine leaves, and then with a dish. Fill up the kettle with water, and let them hang over a slow fire till nest morning, but do not allow the water to boil. Next day, take them out, cool them, and repeat the process with fresh vine leaves, till the cucumbers are a fine green. When cold drain them, cut a small piece out of the flat side, and extract the seeds. Wipe the cucumbers in a dry cloth, and season the inside with a mixture of bruised mace and grated lemon-peel. Tie on with a packthread the bit that was cut out.

Weigh them, and to every pound of cucumbers allow a pound of loaf-sugar. Put the sugar into a preserving kettle, a half pint of water to each pound, and the beaten white of an egg to every four pounds. Boil and skim the sugar till quite clear, adding sliced ginger and lemon parings to your taste. When cool, pour it over the cucumbers, and let them lie in it two days, keeping them covered with a plate, and a weight on it to press it down. Then boil up the syrup again, adding one-half as much sugar, &c. as you had at first; and at the last the juice and grated peel of two lemons for every six cucumbers. The lemon must boil in the syrup but ten minutes. Then strain the syrup all over the cucumbers, and put them up in glass jars.

If they are not quite clear, boil them in a third syrup.

Small green melons may be preserved in this manner.

APPLE RICE PUDDING.

Wash half a pint of rice and boil it till soft and dry. Pare, core, and cut up six large juicy apples, and stew them in as little water as possible. When they are quite, tender, take them out, and mash them with six tablespoonfuls of brown sugar. When the apples and rice are both cold, mix them. together. Have ready five eggs beaten very light, and add them gradually to the other ingredients, with five or six drops of essence of lemon, and a grated nutmeg. Or you may substitute for the essence, the grated peel and the juice of one large lemon. Beat the whole very hard after it is all mixed; tie it tightly in a cloth, (leaving but a very small space for it to swell,) and stopping up the tying place with a lump of flour moistened to paste with water. Put it into a pot of boiling water, and boil it fast for half an hour. Send it to table hot, and eat it with sweetened cream, or with beaten butter and sugar.

BAKED APPLE DUMPLINGS.

Take large, fine, juicy apples, and pare and core them, leaving them as whole as possible. Put them into a kettle with sufficient water to cover them, and let them parboil a quarter of an hour. Then take them out, and drain them on a sieve. Prepare a paste in the proportion of a pound of butter to two pounds of flour, as for plain pies. Roll it out into a sheet, and cut it into equal portions according to your number of apples. Place an apple on each, and fill up the hole from whence the core was extracted with brown sugar moistened with lemon-juice, or with any sort of marmalade. Then cover the apple with the paste, closing it neatly. Place the dumplings side by side in buttered square pans, (not so as to touch,) and bake them of a light brown. Serve them warm or cool, and eat them with cream sauce.

They will be found very good.

INDIAN LOAF CAKE.

Mix a tea-cup full of powdered white sugar with a quart of rich milk, and cut up in the milk two ounces of butter, adding a salt-spoonful of salt. Put this mixture into a covered pan or skillet, and set it on coals till it is scalding hot. Then take it off, and scald with it as much yellow Indian meal (previously sifted) as will make it of the consistence of thick boiled mush. Beat the whole very hard for a quarter of an hour, and then set it away to cool.

While it is cooling, beat three eggs very light, and stir them gradually into the mixture when it is about as warm as new milk. Add a tea-cup full of good strong yeast, and beat the whole another quarter of an hour—for much of the goodness of this cake depends on its being long and well beaten. Then have ready a turban mould or earthen pan with a pipe in the centre, (to diffuse the heat through the middle of the cake.) The pan must be very well buttered, as Indian meal is apt to stick. Put in the mixture, cover it, and set it in a warm place to rise. It should be light in about four hours. Then bake it two hours in a moderate oven. When done, turn it oat with the broad surface downwards, and send it to table hot and whole. Cut it into slices, and eat it with butter.

This will be found an excellent cake. If wanted for breakfast, mix it, and set it to rise the night before. If properly made, standing all night will not injure it. Like all Indian cakes, (of which this is one of the best,) it should be eaten warm.

It will be much improved by adding to the mixture, a salt-spoon of pearl-ash, or sal-aratus, dissolved in a little water.

PLAIN CIDER CAKE.

Sift into a large pan a pound and a half of flour, and rub into it half a pound of butter. Mix in three-quarters of a pound of powdered white sugar and melt a small tea-spoonful of sal-aratus or pearl-ash in a pint of the best cider. Pour the cider into the other ingredients while it is foaming, and stir the whole very hard. Have ready a buttered square pan, put in the mixture, and set It immediately in a rather brisk oven. Bake it an hour or more, according to its thickness. This is a tea cake, and should be eaten fresh. Cut it into squares, split and butter them.

TENNESSEE MUFFINS.

Sift three pints of yellow Indian meal, and put one-half into a pan and scald it. Then set it away to get cold. Beat six: eggs, whites and yolks separately. The yolks must be beaten till they become very thick and smooth, and the whites till they are a stiff froth, that stands alone. When the scalded meal is cold, mix it into a batter with the beaten yolk of egg, the remainder of the meal, a salt-spoonful of salt, and, if necessary, a little water. The batter must be quite thick. At the last, stir in, lightly and slowly, the beaten white of egg. Grease your muffin rings, and set them in an oven of the proper heat; put in the batter immediately, as standing will injure it.

Send them to table hot; pull them open, and eat them with butter.

HOE CAKE.

Beat the whites of three eggs to a stiff froth, and sift into a pan a quart of wheat flour, adding a salt-spoon of salt. Make a hole in the middle, and mix in the white of egg so as to form a thick batter, and then add two table-spoonfuls of the best fresh yeast. Cover it, and let it stand all night. In the morning, take a hoe-iron (such as are made purposely for cakes) and prop it before the fire till, it is well heated. Then flour a tea-saucer, and filling it with batter, shake it about, and clap it to the hoe, (which must be previously greased,) and the batter will adhere, till it is baked. Repeat this with each cake. Keep them hot, and eat them with butter.

MILK TOAST.

Boil a pint of rich milk, and then take it off, and stir into it a quarter of a pound of fresh butter, mixed with a small table-spoonful of flour. Then let it again come to a boil. Have ready two deep plates with half a dozen slices of toast in each. Pour the milk over them hot, and keep them covered till they go to table. Milk toast is generally eaten at breakfast.

POTATO YEAST.

Pare half a dozen middle-sized potatoes, and boil them in a quart of soft water, mixed with a handful of hops, till quite soft. Then mash the potatoes smooth, not leaving in a single lump. Mix with them a handful of wheat flour. Set a sieve over the pan in which you have the flour and mashed potatoes, and strain into them the hop-water in which they were boiled. Then stir the mixture very hard, and afterwards pass it through a cullender to clear it of lumps. Let it stand till it is nearly cold. Then stir in four table-spoonfuls of strong yeast, and let it stand to ferment. When the foam has sunk down in the middle, (which will not be for several hours,) it is done working. Then put it into a stone jug and cork it. Set it in a cool place.

This yeast will be found extremely good for raising home-made bread.

Yeast when it becomes sour may be made fit to use by stirring into it a little sal-aratus, or pearl-ash, allowing a small tea-spoonful to a pint of yeast. This will remove the acidity, and improve the bread in lightness. The pearl-ash must be previously melted in a little lukewarm water.

CREAM CHEESE.

The cheese so called (of which numbers are brought to Philadelphia market) is not in reality made of cream, but of milk warm from the cow, and therefore unskimmed.

Having strained into a tub a bucket of new milk, turn it in the usual way with rennet water. When it has completely come, take a clean linen cloth and press it down upon the firm curd, so as to make the whey rise up over it. As the whey rises, dip it off with a saucer or a skimming dish. Then carefully put the curd (as whole as possible) into a cheese hoop, or mould, which for this purpose should be about half a foot deep, and as large round as a dinner plate—first spreading a clean wet cloth under the curd, and folding it (the cloth) over the top. Lay a large brick on it, or something of equivalent weight, and let the whey drain gradually out through the holes at the bottom of the mould. It must not be pressed hard, as when finished a cream cheese should be only about the consistence of firm butter. The curd will sink gradually in the mould till the whole mass will be about two or three inches thick. Let it remain in the mould six hours, by which time the whey should cease to exude from it. Otherwise, it must be left in somewhat longer.

When you take out the cheese, rub it all over with a little lard, and sprinkle it slightly with fine salt. Set it in a dry dark place, and in four or five days it will be fit for use. When once cut, it should (if the weather is warm) be eaten immediately; but if uncut, it will keep a week in a cold place, provided it is turned three or four times a day. Send it to table whole on a large plate, and cut it when there into wedge-shaped pieces as you would a pie. It is usually eaten at tea or supper, and is by most persons considered a delicacy.

ALMOND BREAD.

Blanch, and pound in a mortar, half a pound of shelled sweet almonds till they are a smooth paste, adding rose-water as you pound them. They should be done the day before they are wanted. Prepare a pound of loaf-sugar finely powdered, a tea-spoonful of mixed spice, (mace, nutmeg, and cinnamon,) and three-quarters of a pound of sifted flour. Take fourteen eggs, and separate the whites from the yolks. Leave out seven of the whites, and beat the other seven to a stiff froth. Beat the yolks till very thick and smooth, and then beat the sugar gradually into them, adding the spice. Next stir in the white of egg, then the flour, and lastly the almonds. You may add twelve drops of essence of lemon.

Put the mixture into a square tin pan, (well buttered,) or into a copper or tin turban-mould, and set it immediately in a brisk oven. Ice it when cool. It is best if eaten fresh. You may add a few bitter almonds to the sweet ones.

CUSTARD CAKES.

Mix together a pound of sifted flour and a quarter of a pound of powdered loaf-sugar. Divide into four a pound of fresh butter; mix one-fourth of it with the flour, and make it into a dough. Then roll it out, and put in the three remaining divisions of the butter at three more rollings. Set the paste in a cool place till the custard is ready. For the custard, beat very light the yolk only of eight eggs, and then stir them gradually into a pint of rich cream, adding three ounces of powdered white sugar, a grated nutmeg, and ratafia, peach-water, or essence of lemon, to your taste. Put the mixture into a deep dish; set it in an iron baking pan or a Dutch oven half full of boiling water, and bake it a quarter of an hour. Then put it to cool.

In the mean time roll out the paste into a thin sheet; cut it into little round cakes about the size of a dollar, and bake them on flat tins. When they are done, spread some of the cakes thickly with the custard, and lay others on the top of them, making them fit closely in the manner of lids.

You may bake the paste in patty-pans like shells, and put in the custard after they come out of the oven. If the custard is baked in the paste, it will be clammy and heavy at the bottom.

They are sometimes called cream cakes or cream tarts.

HONEY GINGER CAKE.

Rub together a pound of sifted flour and three-quarters of a pound of fresh butter. Mix in, a tea-cup of fine brown sugar, two large table-spoonfuls of strong ginger, and (If you like them) two table-spoonfuls of carraway seeds. Having beaten five eggs, add them to the mixture alternately with a pint of strained honey; stirring in towards the last a small tea-spoonful of pearl-ash, that has been melted in a very little water.

Having beaten or stirred the mixture long enough to make it perfectly light, transfer it to a square iron or block-tin pan, (which must be well buttered,) put it into a moderate oven, and bake it an hour or more, in proportion to its thickness.

When cool, cut it into squares. It is best if eaten fresh, but it will keep very well a week.

ROCK CAKE.

Blanch three-quarters of a pound of shelled sweet almonds, and bruise them fine in a mortar, but not to a smooth paste as for maccaroons. Add, as you pound them, a little rose-water. Beat to a stiff froth the whites of four eggs, and then beat in gradually a pound of powdered loaf-sugar. Add a few drops of oil of lemon. Then mix in the pounded almonds. Flour your hands, and make the mixture into little cones or pointed cakes. Spread sheets of damp, thin, white paper on buttered sheets of tin, and put the rock cakes on it, rather far apart. Sprinkle each with powdered loaf-sugar. Bake them of a pale brown, in a brisk oven. They will be done in a few minutes.

When cold, take them off the papers.

FROZEN CUSTARD.

Slice a vanilla bean, and boil it slowly in half a pint of milk/till all the strength is extracted and the milk highly flavoured with the vanilla. Then strain its and set it aside. Mix a quart of cream and a pint of milk, or, if you cannot procure cream, take three pints of rich milk, and put them into a skillet or sauce-pan. Set it on hot coals, and boil it. When it has come to a boil, mix a table-spoonful of flour in three table-spoonfuls of milk, and stir it info the boiling liquid. Afterwards add two eggs, (which have been beaten up with two table-spoonfuls of milk,) pouring them slowly into the mixture. Take care to stir it all the time it is boiling. Five minutes after, stir in gradually half a pound of powdered loaf-sugar, and then the decoction of vanilla. Having stirred it hard a few moments, take it off the fire, and set it to cool. When quite cold, put it into a mould and freeze it, as you would ice-cream, for which it frequently passes.

You may flavour it with a tea-spoonful of strong oil of lemon, stirred in just before you take it from the fire, or with a quarter of a pound of shelled bitter almonds, blanched, pounded in a mortar with a little water, and then boiled in half a pint of milk, till the flavour Is extracted.

CHERRY CORDIAL.

Take a bushel of fine ripe cherries, either red or black, or mixed; stone them, put them into a clean wooden vessel, and mash them with a mallet or beetle. Then boil them about five minutes, and. strain the juice. To each quart of juice allow a quart of water, a pound of sugar, and a quart of brandy. Boil in the water (before you mix it with the juice) two ounces of cloves, and four ounces of cinnamon; then strain out the spice. Put the mixture into a stone jug, or a demijohn, and cork it tightly. Bottle it in two or three months.

COMMON ICE CREAM.

Split into pieces a vanilla bean, and boil it in a very little milk till the flavour is well extracted; then strain it. Mix two table-spoonfuls of arrow-root powder, or the same quantity of fine powdered starch, with just sufficient cold milk to make it a thin paste; rubbing it till quite smooth. Boil together a pint of cream and a pint of rich milk; and while boiling stir in the preparation of arrow-root, and the milk in which the vanilla has been boiled. When it has boiled hard, take it off, stir in half a pound of powdered loaf-sugar, and let it come to a boil again. Then strain it, and put it into a freezer placed in a tub that has a hole in the bottom to let-out the water; and surround the freezer on all sides with ice broken finely, and mixed with coarse salt. Beat the cream hard for half an hour. Then let it rest; occasionally taking off the cover, and scraping down with a long spoon the cream that slicks to the sides. When it is well frozen, transfer it to a mould; surround it with fresh salt and ice, and then freeze it over again.

If you wish to flavour it with lemon instead of vanilla, take a large lump of the sugar before you powder it, and rub it on the outside of a large lemon till the yellow is all rubbed off upon the sugar. Then, when the sugar is all powdered, mix with it the juice.

For strawberry ice cream, mix with the powdered sugar the juice of a quart of ripe strawberries squeezed through a linen cloth.

PINK CHAMPAGNE JELLY.

Beat half the white of an egg to a stiff froth, and then stir it hard into three wine-glasses of filtered water. Put twelve ounces of the best double-refined loaf-sugar (powdered fine and sifted) into a skillet lined with porcelain. Pour on it the white of egg and water, and stir it till dissolved. Then add twelve grains of cochineal powder. Set it over a moderate fire, and boil it and skim it till the scum ceases to rise. Then strain it through a very fine sieve. Have ready an ounce and a half of isinglass that has been boiled in a little water till quite dissolved. Strain it, and while the boiled sugar is lukewarm mix it with the isinglass, adding a pint of pink champagne and the juice of a large lemon. Run it through a linen bag into a mould. When it has congealed so as to be quite firm, wrap a wet cloth round the outside of the mould, and turn out the jelly into a glass dish; or serve it broken up, in jelly glasses, or glass cups. Jelly may be made in a similar manner of Madeira, marasquin, or noyau.

A CHARLOTTE RUSSE.

Boil in half a pint of milk a split vanilla bean, till all the flavour is extracted. Then strain the milk, and when it is cold stir into it the yolks of four beaten eggs, and a quarter of a pound of powdered loaf-sugar.

Simmer this custard five minutes over hot coals, but do not let it come to a boil. Then set it away to cool. Having boiled an ounce of the best Russian isinglass in a pint of water till it is entirely dissolved and the water reduced to one-half, strain it into the custard, stir it hard, and set it aside to get quite cold.

Whip to a stiff froth a quart of rich cream, taking it off in spoonfuls as you do it, and putting it to drain on an inverted sieve. When the custard is quite cold, (but not yet set or congealing,) stir the whipt cream gradually into it.

Take at circular mould of the shape of a drum, the sides being straight. Cut to fit it two round slices from the top and bottom of an almond sponge-cake; glaze them with white of egg, and lay one on at the bottom of the mould, reserving the other for the top.

Having thus covered the bottom, line the sides of the mould with, more of the sponge-cake, cut into long squares and glazed all over with white of egg. They must be placed so as to stand up all round—each wrapping a little over the other so as to leave not the smallest vacancy between; and they must be cut exactly the height of the mould, and trimmed evenly. Then fill up with the custard and cream when it is just beginning to congeal; and cover the top with the other round slice of cake.

Set the mould in a tub of pounded ice mixed with coarse salt; and let it remain forty minutes, or near an hour. Then turn out the Charlotte on a china dish. Have ready an icing, made in the usual manner of beaten white of egg and powdered sugar, flavoured with essence of lemon. Spread it smoothly over the top of the Charlotte, which when the icing is dry will be ready, to serve. They are introduced at large parties, and it is usual to have two or four of them.

A CHARLOTTE POLONAISE.

Boil over a slow fire a pint and a half of cream. While it is boiling have ready six yolks of eggs, beaten up with two table-spoonfuls of powdered arrow-root, or fine flour. Stir this gradually into the boiling cream, taking care to have it perfectly smooth and free from lumps. Ten minutes will suffice for the egg and cream to boil together. Then divide the mixture by putting it into two separate sauce-pans.

Then mix with it, in one of the pans, six ounces of chocolate scraped fine, two ounces of powdered loaf-sugar, and a quarter of a pound of maccaroons, broken up. When it has come to a hard boil, take it off, stir it well, pour it into a bowl, and set it away to cool.

Have ready, for the other sauce-pan of cream and egg, a dozen bitter almonds, and four ounces of shelled sweet almonds or pistachio nuts, all blanched and pounded in a mortar with rose-water to a smooth paste, and mixed with an ounce of citron also pounded. Add four ounces of powdered sugar; and to colour it green, two large spoonfuls of spinach juice that has been strained through a sieve. Stir this mixture into the other half of the cream, and let it come to a boil. Then put it aside to cool.

Cut a large sponge-cake into slices half an inch thick. Spread one slice thickly with the chocolate cream, and cover another slice with the almond cream. Do this alternately (piling them evenly on a china dish) till all the ingredients are used up. You may arrange it in the original form of the sponge-cake before it was cut, or in a pyramid. Have ready the whites of the six eggs whipped to a stiff froth, with which have been gradually mixed six ounces of powdered sugar, and twelve drops of oil of lemon. With a spoon heap this meringue (as the French call it) all over the pile of cake, &c., and then sift powdered sugar over it. Set it in a very slow oven till the outside becomes a light brown colour.

Serve it up cold, ornamented according to your taste.

If you find the chocolate cream too thin, add more maccaroons. If the almond cream is too thin, mix in more pounded citron. If either of the mixtures is too thick, dilute it with more cream.

This is superior to a Charlotte Russe.

APPLE COMPOTE.

Take large ripe pippin apples. Pare, core, and weigh them, and to each pound allow a pound of fine loaf-sugar and two lemons. Parboil the apples, and then set them out to cool. Pare off very nicely with a penknife the yellow rind of the lemons, taking care not to break it; and then with scissors trim the edges to an even width all along. Put the lemon-rind to boil in a little sauce-pan by itself, till it Becomes tender, and then set it to cool. Allow half a pint of water to each pound of sugar; and when it is melted, set it on the fire in the preserving kettle, put in the apples, and boil them slowly till they are clear and tender all through, but not till they break; skimming the syrup carefully. After you have taken out the apples, add the lemon-juice, put in the lemon-peel, and boil it till quite transparent. When the whole is cold, put the apples with the syrup into glass dishes, and dispose the wreaths of lemon-peel fancifully about them.

www.ingramcontent.com/pod-product-compliance
Lightning Source LLC
Chambersburg PA
CBHW080615110526
44587CB00040BB/3526